Worldly Wisdom
and Foolish Grace

Worldly Wisdom and Foolish Grace

Lessons from Abraham's Tent

BARBARA CARNEGIE CAMPBELL

Forewords by Arif Humayun and Batya Podos

RESOURCE *Publications* • Eugene, Oregon

WORLDLY WISDOM AND FOOLISH GRACE
Lessons from Abraham's Tent

Copyright © 2020 Barbara Carnegie Campbell. All rights reserved. Except for brief quotations in critical publications or reviews, no part of this book may be reproduced in any manner without prior written permission from the publisher. Write: Permissions, Wipf and Stock Publishers, 199 W. 8th Ave., Suite 3, Eugene, OR 97401.

Resource Publications
An Imprint of Wipf and Stock Publishers
199 W. 8th Ave., Suite 3
Eugene, OR 97401

www.wipfandstock.com

PAPERBACK ISBN: 978-1-7252-7021-3
HARDCOVER ISBN: 978-1-7252-7020-6
EBOOK ISBN: 978-1-7252-7022-0

Manufactured in the U.S.A. 07/31/20

New Revised Standard Version Bible, copyright © 1989 National Council of the Churches of Christ in the United States of America. Used by permission. All rights reserved worldwide.

Sacred Writings: The Tanakh, copyright © 1985 by The Jewish Publication Society.

Introduction copyright © 1992 by Jaroslave Pelican. Used by permission. All rights reserved.

The Study Quran, copyright © 2015 by Seyyed Hossein Nasr. Used as permitted. All right reserved.

This study is dedicated to
my Mom and Dad,
Joyce and Orris Carnegie.
Their memory is a blessing,
for they lived community, courage, and compassion.

Contents

Foreword by Arif Humayun | ix
Foreword by Batya Podos | xiii
Preface | xix
Acknowledgements | xxiii
Abbreviations | xxv

Introduction | 1
1. It All Belongs To God | 21
2. Children Will Lead Us | 36
3. Plant Seeds and Tend the Soil | 49
4. Love Fulfills the Law | 61
5. Season Passion With Compassion | 74
6. Be a Good Neighbor | 86
7. Turn the Other Cheek | 102
8. Love and Bless Your Enemies | 115
9. Live Generously | 130
10. Let Your Light Shine | 142
Addendum | 153

Bibliography | 155

Foreword

BARBARA CAMPBELL'S APPROACH TO Comparative Religion—seeking similarities and not highlighting "differences" between Semitic faiths in a multicultural and multi-religious society—is commendable. Fortunately, we have moved beyond medieval times when religions and religious thoughts were evolving and the clergy adopted a defensive and exclusive approach through which they could monopolize salvation, condemning other faith traditions as inferior and evil. This exclusive approach was used to control people's thought for power as well as financial and political gains.

During this time, religiously motivated wars were justified and religious fervor was used as a motivator for people to fight in the cause of their faith which was "under threat". These conflicting and, at times, contradictory beliefs of the various religions created a highly confused state in the human mind which can only be resolved by an objective understanding and unbiased analysis of the history, goals, and the teachings of different religions. The net result was that religious traditions prevented people from developing intellectually as they were confined to their respective dogmas.

In the Christian tradition, for example, development in Europe occurred after the Renaissance (15th century) and Reformation (16th century), movements when Christians rejected the Catholic dogma and freed themselves of the clergy-imposed restrictions. This rejection gave birth to the Protestant Church and led to the Industrial Revolution which transformed Western societies and cultures. Similar movements occurred in the Jewish faith and continue to happen among Muslims, resulting in sectarian divisions.

Interestingly, the Muslim transformation has followed a reverse transition in the sense that rational thought became prevalent among Muslims in the 8th century, shortly after the advent of Islam in the 7th century. This Golden Age of Muslims began during the reign of the Abbasid caliph Harun al-Rashid (786 to 809) who allowed free thinking and did not monopolize salvation. He established the House of Wisdom in Baghdad where scholars from various parts of the world, with different religious and cultural backgrounds, were mandated to gather and translate the world's classical knowledge into Arabic and Persian.[1] Consequently, Muslims quickly rose as the unrivalled economic and military power in the world which lasted several centuries. This period is traditionally said to have ended with the collapse of the Abbasid caliphate due to Mongol invasions and the Siege of Baghdad in 1258.[2]

As industrial developments occurred in Europe, Europeans ventured out to other continents in search of raw materials and markets to satisfy the needs of their emerging industries. Technology evolved and Europeans developed and modernized their armies and naval fleets to battle the Muslim Empires (Ottoman, Mughal) who, as leading military and economic powers in the world, were unaware of the changes in Europe and did not feel the need to modernize like the Europeans.

The Muslim Empires were eventually defeated, and their lands colonized. Rejecting rationality, the Muslim clergy filled the leadership vacuum in the colonized empires, citing God's wrath as the cause of defeat and declared Islam to be in danger from the West; the politicized clergy led the Muslims towards dogma as they defined it for political expediency.

This decline in rational thought among Muslims started earlier, in the 14th century; dogmatic control was completed after the defeat of the Ottoman Empire in 1924. Several orthodox Muslim sects and "reformers" have since appeared and attracted disenfranchised Muslims towards their dogma. Dogma-led religious groups, in all traditions, discourage free thinking and prohibit discussion and rationalization of their teachings, encouraging believers to accept simplistic and even illogical explanation as faith.

Geopolitics, the cold war between the US and USSR, and the regional power struggle between Saudi Arabia and Iran have fueled and funded this dogmatic rivalry among Muslims. The 11 September 2001 terrorist attack has been a pivotal point in Muslims' radical dogma; many Muslims are now attempting to find rational approaches to the issues at hand.

Unfortunately, the Muslim dogma, initially developed in the 14th and 15th centuries and reinforced, relatively unchecked, for the next two

---

1. Vartan Gregorian, "Islam: A Mosaic, Not a Monolith", Brookings Institution Press, 2003, pp. 26–38 ISBN 0-8157-3283-X

2. *Islamic Radicalism and Multicultural Politics.* Taylor & Francis. 2011-13-01. p. 9. ISBN 978-1-136-95960-8. Retrieved 26 August 2012.

centuries, was developed when the global economic system was agrarian. It has been difficult to transform the long-held, agrarian-era dogma with a rational understanding of the industrial era, especially in the light of low literacy levels and lack of economic development in the Muslim world. The only source of news, for many Muslims, is their local cleric or mosque who are often funded by some established sectarian and politicized entity who must defend their existence.

Muslim political clergy discredit any reformer by labelling them as a puppet, a traitor, or non-Muslim! The average Muslim is not informed or bold enough to challenge the radicalized clergy in view of the blasphemy and apostasy legislations in many Muslim countries where people are lynched by mobs for such allegations; these "crimes" also carry mandatory capital punishment.

People have thus evolved in "dogmatic silos" which Barbara Campbell is trying to break within the Semitic faiths by explaining the similarities in teachings of their scriptures—Old and New Testaments and the Qur'an—in chronological order. This is a sensible approach as the three Semitic faiths agree on their common origin—Prophet Abraham.

Barbara's idea of Abraham's Tent—a summer camp to bring together school children from the Jewish, Christian, and Muslim traditions—was a successful attempt to break these dogmatic silos by demonstrating the commonalities between these faiths to impressionable and inquisitive minds. Sadly, dogmatic differences among the faiths, and within each faith, may have prevented this idea from blossoming further than it did. Maybe, the idea was ahead of its time!

There are two unintended consequences of growing within dogmatic silos: (1) the intellectual confusion when inquisitive minds fail to rationalize the major "differences" between faiths, and (2) the ease with which propaganda and hateful messages can grow in societies. Exiting these silos enables individuals to understand the big picture and empowers them to challenge propaganda and check the spread of malicious and hateful messages. In the absence of appropriate and rational explanations, the intellectual confusion causes people to drift further away from God and reject religion.

I have similarly researched the origins and commonalities among the Semitic Faiths and attempted to find evolving and common threads between scriptural prophecies. This research started after a Christian colleague in Australia—where I lived for three years—started emphasizing the superiority of Christianity over Islam.

Foreword

Having studied at a Catholic high school, I was familiar with Christianity but, like majority of Muslims, lacked the knowledge and confidence to start a meaningful discussion on Islam. He accepted my proposal that we agree on common questions regarding our respective concerns about the other faith and attempt to find answers to these questions from our respective scriptures. The resultant literature search resulted in the publication of my first book.[3]

Surprisingly, and consistent with Barbara's approach, this research showed a strong evolutionary trend among the prophecies in the Semitic scriptures—the Old and New Testaments and the Qur'an.

My premise for this research was to explore two possible options: Either believe that there are several Gods in the world, each guiding their chosen group of people in different directions or believe that there is one God Almighty who has revealed Himself to all people at different times, but that the message of this one God has been misinterpreted.

The first assumption is absurd and is unanimously rejected by all major religions. For this assumption to be valid, it must be accepted that humans are involved in a "War of Gods", the resolution of which is beyond human control. It is simply inconceivable to visualize a multitude of Gods controlling competing sections of humankind.

The second assumption appears reasonable; I followed this approach to determine any connection between the Semitic scriptures. The validity of this assumption entails that: (1) God is Almighty, All-knowing, Just, Wise, Compassionate, Merciful, Forgiving, Loving, and the ultimate power in every matter, and (2) the basic laws of nature are perfect, uniform and consistent. Our understanding of these laws is imperfect, has evolved with time and our understanding of science. The Perfect God does not need to break, bend or modify His laws to reveal His presence to humans whom he created out of compassion. That compassionate God cannot send conflicting messages to humankind.

Today, while religion has become a mere tool for gaining political control and is exploited by opportunists to achieve personal and political goals, the common message of all religions is to gradually elevate human behavior from the basic instinctive-stage to moral, and ultimately, the spiritual-stage. Religious practices can be regarded as training tools for disciplining

---

3. Arif Humayun, Islam: The Summit of Religious Evolution, Islam International Publications (1992). ISBN Number: 1- 85372 505 6

Foreword

human thought and behavior to become peaceful and loyal citizens, and serving disenfranchised members of the society.

In broad terms, the UN Declaration of Human Rights, adopted in 1948, essentially summarizes the teachings of all religions. The Declaration is a statement of ideals which each faith tradition should aspire to attain. This is the only approach to usher in peace to the world. Interestingly, I have seen a publication where each article of the UN Declaration has been referenced to the Qur'an.[4]

I thus see Barbara Campbell's book as an attempt to demolish the destructive dogmatic silos and enable the reader to broaden their understanding of comparative religion within the Semitic faiths. Bridging this intellectual divide is critical for transforming societies and making religions serve humanity to minimize suffering and usher peace into society.

Arif Humayun
Amaddiyya Mosque, Portland, OR
www.circleofpeaceonline.org

---

4. Muhammad Zafrulla Khan, Islam and Human Rights, Islam International Publications, ISBN: 978-1-84880-862-1

Foreword

THERE IS SOMETHING RARE and remarkable about two diverse communities who operate with one heart. This was the story of P'nai Or of Portland, a Jewish Renewal congregation, and St. Mark Presbyterian Church. P'nai Or, like many small congregations, did not have a building of its own so rented various sites until it found St. Mark. But what began as a landlord/tenant arrangement transformed into a true spiritual partnership.

Both congregations were involved in the Interfaith Council of Greater Portland, congregants from both communities often attended the same events, but when P'nai Or lost their beloved rabbi in an accident, there was a shift. We were not just casual friends sharing the same building. it was the congregation of St. Mark who helped to hold P'nai Or up, who brought them food, who cared for the grieving community. It was the beginning of a transformation that bonded the two communities as spiritual family.

P'nai Or hired an interim rabbi, Rabbi David Zaslow, who came up from Ashland once a month to lead services, teach, and minister to the still grieving congregation. In one of those awkward but ultimately happy coincidences, he came to Portland to lead a Friday night service only to discover that it was Good Friday. What occurred then was nothing short of remarkable, given the trepidation and anxiety with which Jews approach the Easter season.

St. Mark held their Good Friday service and Reb David and the P'nai Or congregation attended, witnessing the grief of the Christian community as that community had witnessed theirs. It was an extraordinary moment, and changed the relationship between the two congregations in their souls. It was impossible for anyone to remain "the other." There were no strangers. There were only brothers and sisters on the same spiritual journey with different experiences and vocabulary.

Foreword

There were classes, dialogues, shared services and events, a kind of intimacy of spirit that even in the interfaith community is not often shared. And from this collaboration of heart and spirit, Abraham's Tent was born, created and mothered by Pastor Barbara Campbell and Maggidah Batya Podos. (A maggid is a storyteller and teacher in the Jewish tradition).

The idea was simple. We should extend the interfaith spirit into a day camp for Jewish, Christian and Muslim children. We already worked with the Ahmadiyya Muslim community and others through the Interfaith Council, why not bring all of Abraham's children together?

After seeking out volunteer teachers from the three communities, and many months of planning, in the summer of 2013 Abraham's Tent was launched. It was a revelation.

The theme was our shared ancestors in the line of Abraham. Held in the Sanctuary, classrooms and on the grounds of St. Mark, each day presented a rotation of learning and experiences from each of the three faiths. As we learned about Abraham's hospitality, snacks were provided by each faith group. As we began to understand our shared roots, we designed paper mural of a massive family tree. As we explored the stories of Isaac and Ishmael, older students created a play about fathers sacrificing their sons. Everyone learned songs in English, Hebrew and Arabic. We played games together. We formed friendships.

On the Friday, we went to the Mosque for a presentation to the Interfaith Council, Friday prayers and snacks. The children got to show what they had learned and created during the week together. The response from the adults was overwhelming.

What we had not expected during this process was that parents needed Abraham's Tent, too. Parent volunteers would gather and talk intensely with each other, so much so that they often forgot they were there to monitor the children. Their interest was such that we discussed having a parent component to the camp, but alas, that never came to be.

We had two years of Abraham's Tent before health issues and circumstance caused Pastor Barbara and Batya (neither in their 20's anymore) to step down from leadership roles. After that, Abraham's Tent ceased to be, but the profound interfaith work with children and families remains.

Pastor Barbara has now retired, the building that housed St. Mark Presbyterian Church has been sold to a college for classrooms, and P'nai Or of Portland has found another home. Yet we are all inspired to continue this

Foreword

work of bringing our sisters and brothers together, to push past divisions and differences, and to encourage us all to be spiritual travelers together.

Batya Podos
Maggidah, Albuquerque, NM

Preface

THEY SAY THAT PREACHERS preach what they most need to hear. I find that to be true. I decided to write this book, when a friend suggested the idea to me, because I knew that there were about ten lessons that Rabbi Jesus taught that I really needed to hear and be reminded of, again and again. I guess I basically wrote this book for me to hold onto, so that I could remember the hardest and truest lessons of the man I consider my Lord and friend.

As it turned out, though the ten hard lessons remained the same, the rest of the writing changed dramatically along the eight or so years that I wrote, put it away, pulled it out, wrote some more, and got distracted again and again by other things in my life. When I had finished ten chapters on the lessons themselves and convinced myself many times that those chapters might actually hold some thoughts others might find interesting, I moved into a transitional period changing the church I would be pastoring, and again the writing ceased for months. When I picked it back up later and looked at it, as I had so many times, I was convinced there was nothing of value there and decided it should not be published. I had sent out one book proposal to one publisher but had not heard back in months.

Then two marvelous things happened. First of all, as I woke up one morning, these words went through my head: "You wrote that book before Trump became POTUS. That's what's wrong with it!" I suddenly began to feel that the lessons were now even more important to share because the present US administration was operating out of the opposite understanding from what Rabbi Jesus taught. A few biblical words from the Apostle Paul (my least favorite biblical author, btw!), got stuck in my head: "Worldly wisdom and foolish grace!"

The other thing that occurred to me was that the book simply had to be more interfaith in nature. I did not really want to assume to be qualified to speak for my Jewish and Muslim brothers and sisters but I had to figure

Preface

out a way to include their voices. The world had suddenly reverted toward a new rise in antisemitism and Islamophobia and it was important to highlight our shared faith tradition.

A few weeks later, I heard from Wipf and Stock Publishers that they actually wanted to publish my book! By the time I wrote back to them accepting their offer, I had to tell them that the book had changed a bit from my original proposal. The title had gone from "Walking With Rabbi Jesus" to "Worldly Wisdom and Foolish Grace: Lessons from Abraham's Tent."

I began to search the lessons and stories from Jewish and Islamic texts that echoed the lessons Rabbi Jesus taught. I knew they were there. My friends had assured me time and again that Rabbi Jesus got his ideas from Torah and that Mohammad (peace be upon him, pbuh) knew both testaments of scripture well. The Elder Testament and Quran are neither short, nor easy writings to search through, however. More than once, I wanted to give up the search. Then, slowly, I began to fill in the pages that begin each chapter with three similar revelations from Abraham's Tent. It was going to work after all!

Having just begun to study Torah and the Quran from my Abrahamic brothers and sisters, I feel unqualified to comment very deeply about the meaning behind these Jewish and Islamic texts. I have included comments by scholars from these traditions and only my brief reflections on these tests. I encourage readers to look more deeply into Torah and Quran and learn from teachers in those traditions. You will find from further study of Torah and Quran that your own faith tradition will also be enlightened.

I wish I could have included similar writings and understandings from all the major world religions and spiritual communities such as Hinduism, Sikhism, Buddhism, Baha'i, Indigenous Spiritual Believers, Pagan and Neo-Pagan groups and Humanism. I would have chosen to include the wisdom of those who do not profess to follow any one faith tradition, but putting together such a study would have taken me at least one more lifetime.

I still feel a bit guilty for not including words from these wise voices, fearing that it might give the idea that I think that Abraham's Tent has a corner on the market of truth and understanding. I wish I could have written more than the brief interpretations that I attempted to add and ask forgiveness from Abraham's Tent members for anything I may have written that is incorrect, misguiding, or offensive. I also ask that anyone from Abraham's Tent contact me and let me know if I have done so, so that I do not spread erroneous information any further.

Preface

I knew that I also had to deal with some of the so-called "Worldly Wisdom". Each of the lessons in the book spoke clearly to one or more current political issue and stood in opposition to the views being espoused by the Trump administration and a growing segment of our culture. Any other view, including the views held by the sacred texts that come out of Abraham's Tent, were suddenly considered "foolishness" by many of our federal leaders.

I also heard the voices of colleagues and wise leaders who fight for justice in my community and around the world, the voices crying out for immigrant justice, the voices of diverse communities facing their own unique forms of prejudice, the voices of those working to save our planet from destruction and desecration, the voices of those pressing against gun violence, child abuse, and so many other forms of violence, fear, and greed. Those voices came to me louder than ever, instigated by the election of Donald Trump as President and subsequent administrative decisions that brought about what still feels like a resurgence of fear, prejudice and extremist nationalism throughout our beloved nation.

I invite you to take a closer look at the current political issues that these lessons throw some light on. I invite you to consider some of the worldly "wisdom" that is spread today. The world claims that their wisdom will make our lives more comfortable, safer, more efficient, and more pleasurable. Is this worldly wisdom truly wise, though?

I must include some disclaimers: I am not a political scientist or cultural sociologist. I listen to as much news as I can stomach and read what I can, but my knowledge is as a complete lay person in this regard. I hope I have been able to simply remind you of some of the social issues we have all been hearing about, so that you can see the stark contrast between how culture and politics view these situations and how people of faith are called to think differently. That contrast and contradiction of views is what makes these ten lessons seem so foolish to our cultural ears. The lessons from Abraham's Tent seem "foolish" because they can only be understood and followed when you stand on a foundation of pure grace, pure unapologetic, undeserved, unconditional grace that allows pure love to flow.

I hope you find it inspiring, remarkable and convicting that these ten important life messages that Rabbi Jesus taught are also shared by Jews and Muslims and, for that matter, by almost every other major world religion. It is also telling that these ten lessons are some of the hardest instructions we will ever hear these great leaders telling us to follow. They are, undoubtedly,

Preface

the lessons that most of the children of Abraham find most difficult to follow. I invite you to reflect bravely and boldly on the "foolish" grace that lies within the opposite and challenging lessons that Abraham's Tent taught throughout the ages and that their disciples continue to believe are possible through living with compassion and humility.

This is not, in the end, your typical "What would Jesus do?" book. Life is complicated and these lessons will not speak to every situation we face today. They might give us a place to start, however. I hope they will encourage us to continue looking and listening for answers that will build the peaceable and beloved community. I hope you will find some comfort and guidance in these texts and be encouraged to continue digging.

I invite you to consider these thoughts just the beginning of a conversation about how we should live in community with others. I hope that you will continue the conversation that this study only begins throughout your life of learning and growing.

It is harder today than ever to speak the words of "foolish grace" to a culture that is filled with the "worldly wisdom" that proclaims hatred, fear, prejudice, violence, conspiracy theories, denial of science and the normalcy of sexism, misogyny, and extremism. My goal is to give you a lens to understand that there are other ways to a greater truth and a more compassionate way to respond.

Go out into the world with courage. The peace of God be with you and hold you tight. These are hard lesson to hear. I know I need to hear them, none-the-less, every day, over and over again. I pray you will give these holy and sacred lessons a chance. I hope you will be able to see and understand beyond my feeble attempts to do these lessons the justice they deserve. I hope you will let them speak to you and move you in a new direction, even if just for a moment, for perhaps we have all been called "to such a time as this." (Esth 4:14)

Acknowledgements

I HAVE RECENTLY STARTED writing down before I get into my bed, at least three things for which I feel grateful. My list of "Gratitude" is in my journal beside my list of "To do" and "Worries." I have found that listing these things makes my mind stop going over it all and let's me fall asleep easily. It's really just turning it all over to a divine spirit that I trust created and cares for me and the entire world day *and* night.

Writing an acknowledgement page is another opportunity, some say, to recognize all for which I am grateful in this one life I've been given. (Other say be short and specific to the book, but that's no fun!) I am most grateful for that loving and mysterious Spirit that I have felt beside and within me since I was a young, introverted child, looking at the world from inside what felt like a box of one way mirrors. I could see out but no one out there could see in. Thanks be to God, for the life of faith I've been led down, a life of unconditional love, grace, and acceptance. I only wish I could have lived it with less worry, which has felt like the greatest sorrow God may have felt about my life.

God has blessed me by being present in the people in my life. My life's journey has brought me to so many people who taught me, through their words and actions, just what I needed to learn. I wish I could mention and thank each of you personally. I pray you know who you are. I have been incredibly fortunate to have walked with the best of the best.

Each of the congregations I was called to serve taught me about pastoring with their gentle assurance and patience. The senior pastors I served beside taught me the things I truly needed to know about ministry. To my beloved church families, you who are too numerous to name, I say, always and forever, "You each have a very special place in my heart."

My dear friends at the P'nai Or Jewish Renewal Congregation and Rizwan Ahmadiyya Mosque not only welcomed me openly and encouraged my

Acknowledgements

questions and stumbling along the path of coming to understand their faith traditions, but made my faith journey whole. Many thanks to my brothers and sisters at P'nai Or: including Rabbi Aryeh, z'tl, Rabbi David, Rabbah Deborah, Cantor Baruck, Magiddahs Batya and Rivkah, mentor Milt, and every one of those "faces of light" who became family to me. Your lives are indeed a blessing to me. To you, always and forever, I say, "Shalom aleichem!"

My dear family at Rizwan Mosque: Harris and Yasemin, Arif and Naila, Shazia, the dear children and youth from Abraham's Tent, and all the dear Rizwan members also welcomed, blessed, and taught me a faith that is so much deeper. To you, always and forever, I say, "as-Salâm Alaikum."

I traveled this interfaith journey as part of the Interfaith Council of Greater Portland. to Kyra, Liathana, David, and all my ICGP friends, thank you for your friendship and dedication to our cause. Angela, you changed my understanding of the faith of The Church of Jesus Christ of Latter Day Saints and my own faith more than any other Christian I know.

Friends leave special marks on our souls. From Laurel, who became my first and lifelong best-friend at the age of five, to Chris, my high school and Girl Scout partner-in-crime, to beloved "Bones" in college, soulmates Rob and Do in seminary, and my weekly coffee/counseling buddies, I am who I am because of your grace-filled spirits and I think of you often with great joy.

This writing would not have been accomplished without the friendship and encouragement of Leas, who first encouraged me to write a book of sermons and kept me at it for lo, these many years. Leas taught me about the Peshita and is a biblical scholar far beyond my pastoral training. He was my first editor, in fact, helping me dig through some of the most difficult passages. Thanks also to the incredibly professional and helpful staff and editors at Wipf and Stock who answered my email-pleas almost daily with patience and support, even during the Covid-19 quarantine.

I am so grateful that I have a family filled with support, laughter, and love. To my siblings and in-laws, my adventurous and loving children: son, Matthew and daughter-in-law Eden, and daughter, Laurel, and the most amazing grandkids Mackey could ever have wished for, thank you for all your love and support every day.

Most of all, to Capi, my lifeline, my partner-in-crime, and my bff! Thank you! Again and again! Without you I'd have missed out on so many historical markers, tiny flowers, birds singing, squirrels playing, moons shining, and the love of many four-legged furry pets!! And, yes, editor Capi, this is obviously too many exclamation points!!

Abbreviations

SCRIPTURE ABBREVIATIONS

Elder Testament

Gen	Genesis
Exod	Exodus
Lev	Leviticus
Num	Numbers
Deut	Deuteronomy
1 Kgs	First Kings
2 Kgs	Second Kings
2 Chr	Second Chronicles
Esth	Esther
Ps (*pl. Pss*)	Psalms
Prov	Proverbs
Isa	Isaiah
Lam	Lamentations
Ezek	Ezekial

Younger Testament

Jas	James
Eph	Ephesians
1 Cor	First Corinthians
Rom	Romans
Matt	Matthew

OTHER ABBREVIATIONS

BCE	Before Common Era
CE	Common Era
GLBTQ	Gay, Lesbian, Bi-sexual, Transgendered, Queer/Questioning
NRSV	New Revised Standard Version
PCUSA	Presbyterian Church in the United States of America
POTUS	President of the United States
Yhwh	Yahweh

Introduction

WORLDLY WISDOM AND FOOLISH GRACE

SAUL OF TARSUS PERSECUTED the followers of Jesus during the early part of the first century CE but had a dramatic change of heart, they say, as he was traveling one day toward the city of Damascus. Christian tradition claims that his name was changed to "Paul" shortly after that experience. Paul became one of the most well-known itinerant preacher and evangelist in the history of Christianity as he spread the message of Jesus to the Gentiles.

Many of the words of Paul and those who worked with him are recorded in the Epistles of the Younger Testament in the form of letters, or *epistles,* to the followers of "the Way," as the first century communities of those who followed Jesus were called. In a letter to followers of "The Way" in the city of Corinth, the man who we now call "The Apostle Paul" wrote about the foolishness of God's grace which stands against the wisdom that the world perceives.

> For the message about the cross is foolishness to those who are perishing, but to us who are being saved it is the power of God. For it is written, "I will destroy the wisdom of the wise, and the discernment of the discerning I will thwart." Where is the one who is wise? Where is the scribe? Where is the debater of this age? Has not God made foolish the wisdom of the world? For since, in the wisdom of God, the world did not know God through wisdom, God decided, through the foolishness of our proclamation, to save those who believe. (1 Cor 1:18–21)

> . . . God chose what is foolish in the world to shame the wise; God chose what is weak in the world to shame the strong; God chose what is low and despised in the world, things that are not, to reduce to nothing things that are. (1 Cor 1:27–28)

Worldly Wisdom and Foolish Grace

Each of the lessons from Abraham's Tent in this book begins with an exploration of what this "worldly wisdom" typically has to say on the subject of that lesson. I am using the phrase "worldly wisdom" in the same way that the Apostle Paul used the phrase, with sarcasm, to refer to the often trusted, taught, and passed down understanding of the secular cultures we live within.

Such "worldly wisdom" is not necessarily truly wise, helpful, or effective. Webster's Ninth Collegiate Dictionary defines "wisdom" as, "1 a: accumulated philosophic or scientific learning: *knowledge* b: ability to discern inner qualities and relationships: *insight* c: good sense: *judgment* 2 a wise attitude or course of action 3:the teachings of the ancient wise men."[1]

"Worldly wisdom" often does not lead to the best ends or the best means, but the "foolish grace" taught by Abraham, Jesus, and Mohammad, peace be upon them, is often exactly the discerning path of understanding that creates real justice and wholeness. Islam respects all prophets equally. A traditional way of showing this respect is to bless the prophets by saying "Peace be upon him (or them)" every time their name/s are spoken or written. I offer this blessing now to all prophets referred to in this study, as a way of blessing them throughout this book while not interrupting the flow of the reading by adding a typed blessing at each reference to a prophet.

The term "foolish grace" was coined when Paul wrote that "the message of the cross is foolishness."(1 Cor 1:18) The message of the cross of Jesus is unmerited, unconditional sacrificial love rather than submission to the injustices of Roman oppression. The cross of Jesus can be summed up as the ultimate metaphor for grace. Webster's Dictionary lists as its first definition of grace, "unmerited divine assistance given man (sic) for his regeneration or sanctification."[2] Grace is the recognition of unmerited gifts which bring peace, wholeness and goodness.

"Foolish grace" points to the fact that such unmerited favor is often seen as unwise or unbelievable by cultural standards. In truth, though it may seem foolish to those whose goal is personal security or betterment and who often believe that there is a scarcity of goods to go around, such "foolish" grace is the way to abundant and true life as opposed to the path of life that is "dead."

During the United States presidential campaign of 2016, the divisions between the right and left wings of religion and culture in our country

1. Merriam, *Ninth*, 1354.
2. Merriam, *Ninth*, 530.

became dramatically deeper and more confusing. What once felt like common etiquette and common, civilized behavior was suddenly ignored in public everywhere.

The moral values that most of us held dear, regardless of which side of the political and religious fences we were on, values such as kindness, compassion, understanding, and caring for others, were threatened; truth seemed to prevail only in the eye of the beholder who began to self-select the truth that fit best for them; the goals of justice and equality were replaced by goals of personal and national wealth, security, and priority.

Although the wisdom of the world is diverse, we once generally felt our particular culture pulling us toward a common understanding of the right way to behave. Instead, we (and our children) are now pulled by media messages, commercials, movies, television, and the conversations of our family, friends, and neighbors to so called "wisdom" that does not improve human life. These messages include ideas such as:

- "You should fear the stranger."
- "You will be happier if you are wealthy and own lots of stuff."
- "You are more lovable if you are young and have a prescribed and preferred body and appearance."
- "You must use violence to protect yourself from your enemies."
- "Women and children are weak and less valuable in our society."
- "People with different speech or skin color or religious belief are dangerous and therefore not to be trusted."

The values of most faith traditions may seem "foolish" to those who trust in the "wisdom" of the world today but we have seen for ourselves, we know from experience, that values such as compassion, nonviolence, and humility are the only forces that have given real success to struggles for peace and justice throughout human history.

LESSONS FROM ABRAHAM'S TENT

The Abrahamic Tradition of faith is often referred to as "the children of Abraham" or "Abraham's tent." Within Abraham's tent we find the faith of three of the major world religions: the faith of the Hebrew people which became, over time, the religion called "Judaism," the faith of those who followed a Judean/Jewish teacher, Jesus of Nazareth, which became known as "Christianity," and the faith of those who followed the revelations of Allah's messenger, the angel Gabriel, to the Prophet Mohammad, which became known as "Islam."

These three "families of faith" within Abraham's tent hold many of the same stories within each of their sacred spiritual texts. The Christian faith grew out of stories and lessons that Jesus told from Torah and other writings that are now part of the Christian Elder Testament. The Quran, God's revelation to the Prophet Mohammad in the seventh century CE, includes many of the stories of Abraham and other Elder Testament prophets, as well as many of the stories of Jesus found in the Younger Testament.

These three faith traditions are monotheistic religions which believe in one creator God. Abraham is credited as the founder of monotheism by all of these faith traditions. Mohammad, in his travels throughout the Middle East as a merchant, met Jews and Christians and heard their faith stories. The story is told that Mohammad may have been so discouraged by the constant conflict and violence between those two religions, which were so closely related, that he continued to listen for a new message from Allah about a more pure form of living faithfully as Allah willed.

Many people who are part of these three faith groups acknowledge today that they worship the same God, the same divine Ground of all Being. There is little disagreement within Abraham's tent today about whether the "foolish grace" of Yahweh/God/Allah and the "wisdom" of the world are often on radically different moral and ethical tracks.

One of the over-arching lenses through which I have studied the scriptures of the Elder and Younger Biblical Testaments and have learned to think theologically is the lens of interfaith understanding, especially the lens of those sharing Abraham's tent. Each chapter in this study will begin with three quotes, listed in chronological order, first a quote from the Elder Testament, then one from the Synoptic Gospels of the Younger Testament, then a quote from the Quran or the Hadith of Islamic traditions.

The Elder Testament quotes are taken from the Tanakh, the English translation completed by The Jewish Publication Society in 1985. "Tanakh" is a word originating from an acronym which represents the three major parts of Hebrew Scripture: t for Torah, n for *nevi'im* or prophets, and k for *kethuvim* or writings.

The Tanakh was first translated into an Aramaic version called the *Targum*. Because many Jews in the Helenistic world spoke Greek, the Tanakh

Introduction

was also quickly translated into a Greek version, called the *Septuagint,* after the "seventy-two" translators who worked on it. Legend has it that each of the seventy-two came up with an identical translation even though they worked separately.³

Unless I include a specific reference in the footnotes, the scripture references taken from the Elder and Younger Testaments of Christian scripture throughout this study will be taken from New Revised Standard Version of the Bible. The New Revised Standard Version (NRSV) was first published in 1989 by the Division of Christian Education of the National Council of the Churches of Christ in the USA. This version replaced the Revised Standard Version which the National Council of Churches had published in 1952.

The spiritual quotes from the Islamic tradition are taken from two sources. I take these quotes from the Quran which contains the revelations the Prophet Muhammad received from God's messenger, the Angel Gabriel; messages which Islam considers the literal word of God. I will be quoting from "The Study Quran" with Editor-in-Chief, Seyyed Hossein Nasr. This is the translation and commentary that sits near my desk at all times.

Islamic quotes will also be taken from "The Wisdom of the Prophet: Sayings of Muhammad" which translates selections from the Hadith, the second most important literary source in Islam, into English. The Hadith do not contain revelations, in the sense that the Quran is considered a complete revelation. Hadith was collected about two centuries after the Prophet's death to document what the Prophet is remembered as saying or doing during his lifetime and relied on people's memories over generations. A rule of thumb in Islam is that if any hadith is contrary to or not supported by the Quran, it cannot be considered valid.

Let me share, a this point, a few stories from my personal faith and interfaith journey. I have spent nearly seven decades listening to and studying stories about the man people call "Jesus of Nazareth" and "Jesus, the Christ." This man, most agree, lived two thousand years ago on the other side of the world. As a child, adults told me stories of Jesus that led me to understand him as a man of compassion, acceptance, and love. As I grew in understanding, I accepted that Jesus uniquely and sacrificially revealed the divine One to me and therefore had "saved" me from all that sought to destroy my life.

---

3. Pelican, *Judaism,* xi-xv.

Later, I began to hear from some Christians that only the followers of Jesus were "saved." Many said he was the only divine son of the one and only God who judged people severely for their mistakes and saved only those who believed in Jesus. Believing in Jesus, many told me, made people "good enough" to go to heaven when they died. Only by God's grace did I refuse (eventually) to believe that the one God was vindictive and violent and continue to know Jesus as one who perfectly revealed a compassionate, forgiving, and grace-filled Creator.

Perhaps it was this conflict between two understandings of Christianity that finally led me to seek a seminary education. I went to learn how to study the words of Christian scripture more deeply so that I could defend and share the compassion and justice of the God I knew and trusted. In a Christian seminary, it was no surprise that as I learned how to study ancient literature most of what I studied was the Younger Testament. I had chosen to attend a progressive seminary within a reformed Christian denomination so that I could study many theologies of the divine other than that of a God who seeks retribution and saves only a chosen few.

When I became an ordained Presbyterian (PCUSA) minister who preached to a congregation regularly, I continued to study the biblical texts that I was called to interpret to others. I read many different interpretations of these stories from many Christian commentaries.

I found the same interpretations repeated almost verbatim again and again in many of these commentaries as if the authors were simply copying each other. Once in a while I found newer research based on what is called "The Search for the Historical Jesus." The theologies of these scholars, who other Christians sometimes considered heretical, began to line up with the Jesus I had known since childhood. The "historical Jesus" spoke less to salvation doctrine and more to how one could live faithfully and in keeping with a divine calling.

In 2003, I became the pastor of St. Mark Presbyterian Church in Portland, Oregon, one of the most progressive Presbyterian Church in the USA (PCUSA) congregations in Oregon, and one of only three open and affirming "More Light" congregations in Cascades Presbytery. I felt I had finally found my people, my tribe, within my life-long PCUSA community. St. Mark had been a founding member, before I became their pastor, of both the Community of Welcoming Congregations of Oregon and the Interfaith Council of Greater Portland.

Introduction

In 2007, a member of a small Jewish Renewal congregation called P'nai Or (which means literally "faces of light") walked into my office at St. Mark asking if her community could rent space in our building on Fridays and Saturdays. Since we were not using the building on those days, our congregation agreed eagerly anticipating, initially, some much needed additional income. It wasn't long, however, before we appreciated even more deeply the relationship that began to develop between P'nai Or and St. Mark and the fact that they could help us reconnect with our Christian roots by teaching us much more about stories within the Elder Testament and Judaism.

We grieved with these brothers and sisters from P'nai Or when their founding rabbi and our friend, Rabbi Aryeh Hirshfied, z'tl died in a tragic scuba diving accident in Mexico in 2009. (*z'tl* is a shortened Hebrew phrase which is transliterated as "His name is a blessing" and is used in the Jewish tradition to show deep respect to those who have died.) St. Mark stood alongside P'nai Or, in compassion and support, at Aryeh's memorial service at St. Mark.

Almost a year later, two amazing experiences brought us even closer together. First of all, Rabbi Zaslow, the Interim Rabbi of P'nai Or at that time, offered to teach a class based on his soon to be published book, *Roots and Branches*. One night each week for six weeks, over sixty people from P'nai Or, St. Mark and other churches in the area, came together in an overcrowded fellowship hall at St. Mark to study with Rabbi David. I took on the assignment from Rabbi David to prime our discussions each week with some of the sticky issues that complicated our Christian/Jewish dialogue.

In this class, Christians and Jews alike began to understand Jesus as a spiritual seeker who had been immersed in the study of Torah. Torah is also called the Pentateuch (from the Greek, *penta*, for five) and refers to the first five books in the Elder Testament which are attributed to Moses. Jesus had been taught the words of Torah since he was a young boy. Most of the words, images and stories that Jesus used in his teachings were learned from Torah. The justice and healing that Jesus worked to create during his lifetime was the justice and healing that he had learned from Torah and had heard the Elder Testament prophets declare to be God's will.

Not long after our shared class, during our Wednesday night choir practice preceding Good Friday, I looked down into the sanctuary from the choir loft and saw that P'nai Or's set up person was preparing the sanctuary for their Friday Shabbat service. St. Mark also planned to be in the

Worldly Wisdom and Foolish Grace

sanctuary at the same time for our Good Friday worship that night. I had forgotten to remind P'nai Or of our Good Friday worship service!

The following morning, I called Rabbi David. He immediately came into the church where we recognized that we had little time to get word out about a change of venue for either group. After considering whether we could simply find separate places in the building for each group to meet, we began wondering if it would be possible to create an experience of worship that would connect spiritually with Christians (who were mourning the crucifixion and death of Jesus) and Jews (who had been blamed for the death of Jesus by Christians for nearly 2,000 years). We knew full well that such a thing had probably never been attempted before but decided we should do what we both felt called by the Spirit to do.

I knew that first of all I had to remove the First Century CE anti-Semitic editorial polemics from the Passion Story of Jesus' arrest and crucifixion that attempted to blame "the chief priests, all the elders, and the people;" and subsequently "all Jews" for the death of Jesus. Some of those anti-Semitic texts are: Matt 26:3–5; 27:1–2, 20–22, 24–25; Mark 14:1–2; 15:1, 6–15, and Luke 22:3–6, 66–71, 23:1–5, 13–23.

As I began to re-translate the offensive words of the Passion Story into phrases that perhaps better reflected the truth of what happened, Rabbi David walked back and forth from my office to the sanctuary where he had continued to pray about whether such an interfaith Good Friday/Passover experience was even possible. When I read him the texts I had revised, he asked me, "Can you do that?" My response was, "It's been retranslated and revised for two thousand years!"

We decided to create a fairly traditional Christian Good Friday worship experience with the P'nai Or congregation being invited to stand with us in our time of mourning with their prayers and worship. We began, however, as the Jewish Shabbat begins every Friday evening, by lighting the two Shabbat candles. Then, as Christians traditionally observe on Maundy Thursday, we observed Communion remembering that the Last Supper of Jesus with his disciples was also the last Passover Seder meal that Jesus shared with his Jewish followers.

Rabbi David prayed the traditional Passover Seder prayers behind the communion table with his arms outstretched and his head covered with his prayer shawl. When his prayers ended and I had offered the traditional Christian words used before communion, Christians came forward to receive the bread and dip it into the common cup of grape juice. Some of the

Introduction

Jews, when invited, also came forward a bit cautiously and tore off a piece of bread from the same loaf and took a small cup of juice from a tray on the table which represented the traditional last cup shared at their annual Seder meal.

Our Jewish brothers and sisters later prayed their ancient Prayer for the Martyrs as the Christians stood around the communion table and lit candles in memory of Jesus. We sang Christian and Jewish songs celebrating the martyrs and mourning the crucifixion of Jesus. We ended with a recitation of Psalm 23 by a ten-year-old girl; a psalm that is read at both Good Friday services and Jewish memorials.

As the service concluded, the Christians left mourning the death of Jesus at the hands of those Romans and Judeans in power who feared his message and popularity. St. Markers left in silence, walking behind the still-burning Christ Candle that I carried out of the darkened sanctuary.

Seven Tenebrae candles had shared the communion table that evening with the two Shabbat candles. The Tenebrae candles had been extinguished one by one following each lesson telling the story of Jesus' death. As St. Markers and P'nai Or members came out mingled together into the foyer some turned around and looked back into the dark sanctuary and saw only the two Sabbath candles still burning, candles which represent, in the Jewish tradition, the kingdom of God still to come in fullness to the world.

The Jews left the sanctuary that night mourning the death of one of their great Judean teachers and prophets. Thousands of other Judeans had also died on crosses that hung on the roads leading in and out of Jerusalem during those years; thousands of others had been crucified, like Jesus, suspected of acts of sedition against Rome. It was clear to all of us that there was a serendipitous, holy spirit present that Good Friday Shabbat evening that embraced, comforted and led each of us to new depths of faith.

As Christians typically do after Good Friday services, members of St. Mark left the foyer directly that evening into the parking lot, to drive or walk home silently in the darkness of the night. As Jews do every Friday night after their Shabbat service, the Jewish congregation walked into our fellowship hall for refreshment and conversation. I had gone into my office to disrobe when a member of P'nai Or appeared at my door inviting me to join them in the fellowship hall. When I entered the hall everyone was sitting silently, which was highly unusual for this typically talkative group.

Rabbi David began playing his guitar and P'nai Or joined in singing to me. The memory of that moment still brings tears. I can only tell you a few of the words of their song: "Be not afraid. He walks beside you always . . ." When I asked member of P'nai Or, after the singing, how the worship experience had been for them, they shared feelings like, "You gave us back Rabbi Jesus!" "I finally understand what Easter means," and "I no longer feel angry or blamed for his death."

Our relationship with P'nai Or drew us into even greater interfaith connections in our community. I joined people of many faiths on the Interfaith Council of Greater Portland, an organization formed in Portland, Oregon by three spiritual leaders from Abraham's tent following 9/11.

Rizwan Mosque, not far from St. Mark, is the oldest mosque in Portland and a bit like our missing triplet. Ahmadiyya Muslims, Jewish Renewal Congregations, and More Light Presbyterians are progressive faith communities equally rejected by some traditional members of their own faith traditions.

In 2013, leaders from Rizwan Ahmadiyya Islamic Mosque, P'nai Or, and St Mark decided to plan together for an Abraham's Tent Summer Day Camp for children and youth from our three faith communities. We coordinated and directed the week-long, all day camp jointly for two summers until St. Mark had to give up its building due to financial difficulties. We discovered amazing similarities between our three traditions and within our three sacred texts. One of our day camp adult leaders described the Interfaith Summer Camp experience as an opportunity to build peace in our community:

> In this day and age we find ourselves deeply interconnected through technology. A ten-year-old can connect with anyone around the world with a computer and access to the Internet. She may play a game or post a message on a Facebook page. This kind of interaction, in fact, has become quite common, but what we lack is face-to-face connection. What we lack even more is the opportunity to sit down and reason together with people who think and worship differently. If we did that more often, perhaps we would let go of fear and understand what Abdullah, another youth participant, realized: "I learned that we are all more alike than I thought." Maybe we're concerned about offending. Maybe we don't know where to begin a conversation or don't want to appear ignorant. Interfaith dialogue requires courage, but the alternative, as we have seen (during this summer of violence against strangers), can be tragic. St. Mark, P'Nai Or, and the Ahmadiyya Muslim Community took a chance for one week that some in all three faiths might frown upon. But sixteen children now have a

Introduction

greater knowledge of themselves and the world in which they live after walking through the flaps of Abraham's Tent together. And peace just took a monumental step forward.

As part of Abraham's Tent, Jewish, Christian, and Islamic children and their adult leaders were amazed to learn that the Quran contains many of the stories found in the Elder and Younger Testaments. The message that the Prophet Mohammad delivered to his people, the Quran, is filled with stories about Abraham, Moses, the Prophets, Mary, Jesus, and many other characters found in the Bible. It became clear that we could understand our own sacred texts better as we became more familiar with the other sacred writings from Abraham's tent.

P'nai Or worshipped with St. Mark every year after that on Good Friday and we continued our summer interfaith Abraham's Tent Day Camp until the St. Mark congregation was dissolved due to declining finances. St. Mark members moved on to several other PCUSA congregations in Portland while P'nai Or staying on in the building which they rented from the Presbytery.

During these years, I had the wonderful opportunity to share a small sacred text study with two special friends: Angela, a life-long leader in the Church of Jesus Christ of Latter Day Saints, and Arif, a life-long leader from the Rizwan Ahmadiyya Muslim community. The three of us met monthly having decided ahead of time that we would come with texts, stories or understandings from our own faith tradition that spoke to a certain theme such as peacemaking, ecology, compassion, salvation, prophets, inclusion, or justice. My faith was so enriched and broadened by these conversations and loving friendships.

At the beginning of each chapter in this book, I include epigraphs of sacred texts from Torah, The Younger Testament Gospels and The Quran or Muslim Hadith writings as examples of how all three of these ancient texts reveal the same truth and divine will on how we are to live together.

For the sake of time and convenience through this study, I will call the one divine Ground of all Being, the one divine energy of love and peace that we worship, "God." In my own mind, I sometimes substitute the word "Good" for "God" when I'm trying to see things from the point of view of those of no faith or those whose faith is non-theistic. I do not claim to understand "God," as separate or different in any way from "Adonai," "Allah," or any of the other names people give to their experience of the Holy.

ANCIENT LESSONS FOR TODAY

Jesus, was a Judean religious teacher called, by those who knew him, "Yoshua," a common Hebrew name which would have been pronounced *Yeshua* or *Yehoshua*, in Hebrew. The English names "Jesus" and "Joshua" are derivatives of this common Arabic name.

Jesus lived 2,000 years ago in what is now Israel and Palestine. His words, which many believe are recorded, in some fashion, in the Gospels, are ancient words spoken for people who lived long ago and far away. We live in a time and place that is changing faster than ever. Younger generations are no longer accepting, verbatim, what religious institutions have long been trying to convince others to believe through the literal reading of their ancient texts.

Sharing the good news that Jesus taught is the true definition of "evangelism." Evangelism is usually misunderstood by today's culture. Evidence of this comes even from Webster's Dictionary which includes as its definition of "evangelism" "1: the winning or revival of personal commitments to Christ 2: militant or crusading zeal."[4] News reporters say that 72 percent of white evangelicals support Trump as if 72 percent of all Republicans and other conservative citizens are out there spreading the good news, trying to create or revive commitment to Christ.

It is harder than ever to teach the ancient lessons of Abraham's tent, because fewer and fewer people have heard the stories enough times for the stories to have the same effect on their lives that they have had on others. At one point in history, most tribal life included participation in the rituals and beliefs of the entire tribe. At one time the majority of people in a village shared the same understanding of the God that they worshiped and the direction of the village priest, which dictated every part of their lives with the requirements for going to heaven or hell. Most of the Europeans who came as the first immigrant settlers to North America would have professed to being Christian, even as they became colonizers, killing off those whose land they assumed God had given to them to inhabit because of their faith.

Faith is not as easy to come by as it used to be. Recent generations have been born into a world filled with technologies and scientific understandings far beyond that of the world their parents and grandparents knew. Cultural connections, community relationships and moral perspectives can now be found in many places other than religious centers. And on top of

---

4. Merriam, *Ninth*, 429.

Introduction

this, the hypocrisy, injustice, and violence of many religious traditions has become all too evident.

We live in a different religious culture today. Many changes have taken place throughout the course of human history in the understanding and practice of established religions. Some of these changes took thousands of years to take effect and others, such as the Great Reformation of the 1500s, took little more than a hundred years. With the turn of the twenty first century, not only the United States but other modernized nations began to experience another "reformation" of culture and tradition. Historians predict that the twenty first century will dramatically change not only economic, technological, and social norms, but the theology and practice of our faith traditions as well. Within another hundred years everything will look and work differently around us.

But take heart, if you are a person of faith! Faith is not dying. It is just evolving, as it did 500–600 years ago. That's how human societies seem to operate. Every 500 years most advanced cultures of the world experience a systemic and dynamic change in everything people once held as true, traditional, and trustworthy. New light starts gradually shining on established roles, norms, and expectations during the century preceding these great changes and eventually, even those most unwilling to change eventually do so.

Dr. Phyllis Tickle, a historian, professor and scholar of Christian history and theology, wrote in 2012 about this next wave of great societal change in her book "The Emergence Church:"

> Of the several general characteristics that the Great Emergence and Emergence Christianity hold in common, these of deinstitutionalization; non-hierarchical organization; a comfortable and informed interface with physical science; dialogical and contextual habits of thought; almost universal technological savvy; triple citizenship with its triple loyalties and obligations; a deeply embedded commitment to social justice with an accompanying, though largely unpremeditated, assumption of all forms of human diversity as the norm; and a vocation toward greenness—these undoubtedly are among the most characterizing.[5]

Tickle's book should be "required reading" by any who hope to ride out the wave of the next reformation into a better understanding of what it means to be people of faith and church. What Tickle and other emergent

---

5. Tickle, *Emergence*, 137.

faith leaders are saying to faith communities is that the generations born after the 1970s are more likely to be disillusioned by the hypocrisies of established religions than any generation before them.

Yet, as many who reject religious institutions look for a way to make life better, more just, and more meaningful, many alternate worshipping communities, who draw in Millennials by gathering in brew pubs or coffee shops, are being led by those who preach the same biblical understanding that belief in Jesus alone grants salvation.

Millennials hope to be inspired by goodness and love. Some may feel there is still hope for people of faith, but they are looking for something other than hours spent in worship and charitable giving spent mostly on supporting large facilities and organizations. They are only willing to accept a gospel message which teaches compassion, inclusion, and justice for all.

Many in younger generations are seeking ways to live a life that is loving, kind and just, but are moving away from worshiping deities, especially those who are imagined in human images (theism), and are turning instead toward embracing the teachings of other "light-bearers" so that they can be inspired to act in the world in life-giving ways.

I recently drove by a neighborhood church reader board that asked, "Have your answers to life brought peace to this world? This comes very close to expressing what many people in younger generations are seeking: spiritual answers that bring peace to the world rather than a set of religious beliefs and rules that judge, condemn, and divide us.

I still believe in the God of Abraham whom I have heard stories of since I was a child, but I have grown in my faith and understanding. My faith has changed. Today I trust in a divine force of creation that is a force of good, of light and of love; invisible yet at work in the world; mysterious yet as alive and as real to me as every beat of my heart and every breath I take.

I trust that this divine force formed divinity within all creatures and all creation. After all, it is said that "75 percent of our genetic make-up is the same as a pumpkin."[6] I trust that Jesus and other uniquely spiritual people were so in touch with the divinity within themselves that ordinary people sensed that divinity in unique ways.

---

6. BBC, "Human Genome".

Introduction

HOW THEN SHOULD WE LIVE?

Most of us want to do the right thing, ethically and morally, but life is complicated and it is often quite difficult to figure out what that right thing is. Human nature often distracts us from making the right decision when we try to balance conflicting options.

A popular saying could be found, years ago, written on everything from bracelets to bumper stickers—"What Would Jesus Do?"—or the even more irritating acronym,—*WWJD*? I usually find this catchy question to be about as helpful as lighting a candle in a hurricane when it comes to making faithful, moral decisions. How could anyone ever truly know what someone, who lived 2,000 years ago, would think or do in the twenty-first century? We don't have a perfectly preserved original document of everything Jesus said, thought or did, regardless of what some people believe the Bible to be!

And yet, as unrealistic as this question sounds, those who have heard the stories of Jesus sometimes feel as if Jesus has become a present, living reality in their lives. Such a living relationship enables them to feel that they know, sometimes beyond any doubt, what Jesus would do. The memories and stories of beloved friends, teachers, or other great minds might guide us in the same way.

In the end, to ask ourselves what the persons we respect most would do or say about an issue should help us find answers to the even more important question, "What should *I* do?" When we seek values that will strengthen our common life, ancient spiritual narratives may be a good place to begin. It is important, however, to study these lessons in their appropriate contexts, cultures, and languages. The purpose of studying these ten lessons from Rabbi Jesus, and similar lessons from Jewish and Islamic holy texts, is to help us understand how to best live in accordance with the radically "foolish" compassion and grace they affirm.

STUDYING ANCIENT LITERATURE

It is a complicated, often impossible task to understand, with any level of assurance, what ancient writings may have meant to their original authors and audience. Yet, it's an endeavor and adventure that can lead to treasures beyond measure. A literal treasure hunt usually begins with a map with a spot marked X. We follow the map to that spot where we do lots of digging. In researching ancient texts we must dig through ancient manuscripts written in ancient languages along with endless translations, the perceived historical context in which the text was written, and many other layers of literary and historical information if we hope to find any treasure. We can only hope to get closer to some layer of deeper meaning. The unknown imagination of an often unknown author may prevent us from finding the precious information we seek. Even though we may never discover the entire truth of a particular text, it is worth the digging just to get closer than we once were.

It is important to study ancient texts by looking at the original languages in which the texts were written. English translations of early Aramaic and Greek biblical texts, for instance, often reveal textual translations and interpretative decisions that may not have been totally objective. It is far too easy to read what we expect to read or hope to read into a text we are translating. The study of original languages looks for the interpretive option which seems most appropriate in the originating context and culture.

I will do some of my own such dangerous interpretive work in this study. It is my goal to look behind the familiarity of the English translations to hear the original message in its own language. I am not, however, as trained in these ancient languages as are many scholars. I have relied on only a select few translations into English from the original Aramaic or Greek languages and will not attempt to use original languages in looking at translations from the Tanakh or Quran.

Lacking conclusive evidence about the identity of the author/s of each of the Synoptic Gospels, I will use the name ascribed to the gospel as shorthand for the actual author. For instance, I will use "Matthew", to refer to the unknown author/s of the Gospel of Matthew. This is for the simplification of reading and not because I am assuming that the author's name was actually Matthew.

During my digging for treasures in scripture, I have used many tools of understanding. In terms of Christian scripture, these layers sometimes included:

- an understanding that many texts in the Younger Testament (Gospels and Epistles) are rooted in the Elder Testament (Torah, Prophets, and Wisdom literature),
- an understanding that Jesus and most, but not all, of the other Younger Testament writers were Judeans steeped in Torah, not Jews as we know them today *or* Christians. (Terms which came into use many centuries later.)

Introduction

- an understanding that possible evangelistic polemics could have influenced the retelling of the oral stories passed down to the authors and later work by editors and translators, and
- an understanding that Mohammad's revelation recorded in the Quran is deeply connected with the Abrahamic traditions of both Judaism and Christianity.

Some Christian texts are distorted by shameful anti-Jewish or anti-Semitic sentiments that arose during the centuries following Jesus' death (such as those that we changed for our Good Friday/Passover Worship). Though original writers, editors or translators may have had the best of intentions, they may have been heavily influenced by the fears and prejudices of their time.

It is disturbing, none the less, that some of their words have been used to spread hatred toward our Jewish brothers and sisters since the time of Jesus. It is important to re-translate these texts which misrepresent and misstate the events of Jesus' life, trial and death and developed into the dangerous Christian doctrines of Super-secession-ism, and Replacement Theology.

"Supersecessionism" is the understanding that Christianity supersedes Judaism, that Christianity fulfills Biblical Judaism, and that Jews, therefore, who deny that Jesus was the Jewish Messiah, fall short in their calling as God's chosen people. An even more radical form of Super-secession-ism is "Replacement Theology," which maintains that the Jews are no longer considered God's chosen people because the Christian gospel has replaced the law and commandments of the Jewish people.

Literary scholars use the word "criticism" to describe various techniques used in studying literature. Many different forms of this sort of criticism have been developed to help us interpret the meaning of ancient texts. The major types of biblical criticism include but are not limited to:

a. "textual" criticism which is concerned with establishing the original or most authoritative text,

b. "philological" criticism which is the study of the biblical languages for an accurate knowledge of vocabulary, grammar, and style of the period,

c. "literary" criticism which focuses on the various literary genres embedded in the text in order to uncover evidence concerning date of composition, authorship, and original function of the various types of writing that constitute the specific literature being examined,

d. "tradition" criticism which attempts to trace the development of the oral traditions that preceded written texts,

e. "form" criticism which classifies the written material according to the pre-literary forms, such as parable or hymn,

f. "redaction" criticism which studies how the documents were assembled by their final authors and editors, and

g. "historical" criticism, which seeks to interpret writings in the context of their historical settings.[7]

In the last several decades historical criticism has received special attention in the attempt to discover more about the historical nature of a certain figure, such as Jesus. Historical criticism has led us to what may be the most authentic words these historical figures taught or wrote.

Most scholars of ancient literature use textual, contextual and literary criticism, at least, in deciding which words are most likely the authentic words of their ascribed speaker or author, rather than the interpretation of a later author, who may or may not have known the original speaker or author personally, or the interpretation and polemic of a later editor and/or translator. For instance, if the perceivable date of a text seems to be after the death of the ascribed author or from within a community of which the speaker or author could not have been a part, scholars identify that text as not completely original.

JESUS, A JUDEAN TEACHER

The terms "Rabbi, Jew, Jewish, and Judaism" came into use around the fourth century CE. Most of these terms come from the word "Judean." In the area that is now Israel and Palestine, "Judeans" were the people from lands to the north, also called the tribe of Judah, and "Israelites" were from the south and tribe of Israel. Both tribes worshiped *Yahweh* with only a few differences in their traditions. Over time these two tribes and traditions merged into one people and one faith.

Rabbi David Zaslow who now serves Havurah Shir Hadash, a Jewish Renewal Congregation in Ashland, Oregon, writes this about the Jewishness of Jesus:

---

7. Encyclopedia Brittanica, "Biblical Criticism".

Introduction

> It's easy to utter the words 'Jesus was Jewish,' but more difficult for members of either faith to actually imagine this as an historical reality. Many Christians think of the Jewishness of Jesus in the same way they think of the Catholicism of Martin Luther—in other words, he was a Catholic but he broke away from many of the theological doctrines of the church at that time.
>
> Jesus, however, never left Judaism. Along with other great rabbis that Jews study and revere, . . . Jesus was sometimes critical of the often hypocritical and corrupt Temple priesthood led by the Sadducees. But Jesus never left Judaism, even when he was critical of its hypocrisy. He never abandoned the practice of fulfilling the Torah's commandments.
>
> For the Jews to imagine Rabbi Joshua (Jesus) davvenen (praying) each morning with his talmidim (students) while all are wearing tallit (prayer shawls) and t'fillin (phylacteries) is contrary to two thousand years of Christian art that sought to de-Judaize Jesus and his disciples. [8]

Although the title of "Rabbi" was not used until the fourth century, Jesus is called "Rabboni", which translates as "my teacher," three times in The Younger Testament. I will use the title, "Rabbi Jesus" in this study in deference to both the life Rabbi Jesus led as a Judean teacher and his later Western Christian identity. We must, however, remember that Rabbi Jesus was not the type of rabbi that we know today. Calling Jesus "Rabbi" is helpful only because it helps us remember the culture and religious traditions that he knew and loved.

Rabbi Jesus preached about and interpreted Torah during the beginning of the reforming of the first century CE Judean religion. With the destruction of the Jewish Temple in Jerusalem in 76 CE, temple worship ended and Jewish traditions moved into homes and synagogues. Other well-known religious leaders of this time, such as Hillel, thought and taught in the same vein as Rabbi Jesus.

As the Younger Testament states, Rabbi Jesus probably did not intend to abolish one "stroke of a letter" of the law. (Matt 5:18) He did, however, set his teachings from Torah into new contexts to make them come alive for his contemporary audiences. He created unique, interpretive stories, "midrash," in other words, which had such a powerful impact on his followers that they were included, over a thousand years later, in the Bible as the Younger Testament alongside the Elder Testament of Torah, Prophets, and Wisdom Literature.

8. Zaslow, *Roots*, 12.

Worldly Wisdom and Foolish Grace

I use the terms "Elder" and "Younger" Testaments to remind us that the more common terms "Old" and "New" Testament are offensive to our Jewish brothers and sisters. The term "old" can carry the connotation of something that is no longer preferable or relevant as opposed to the word "new" that connotes something that is "better" and has replaced that which was "old." "Old Testament" and "New Testament" perpetuate the understanding that Christianity somehow replaces or is better than Judaism.

1

It All Belongs To God

When Caesar stamps his image on a coin,
all the coins come out identical.
When the One Who is Beyond All Rulers
stamps the Divine Image on a coin
each coin comes out unique.

SANHEDRIN 38A[1]

Then the Pharisees went and plotted to entrap (Jesus) in what he said. So they sent their disciples to him, along with the Herodians, saying, "Teacher, we know that you are sincere, and teach the way of God in accordance with truth, and show deference to no one; for you do not regard people with partiality. Tell us, then what you think. Is it lawful to pay taxes to the emperor, or not?" But Jesus, aware of their malice, said, "Why are you putting me to the test, you hypocrites? Show me the coin used for the tax." And they brought him a denarius. Then he said to them, "Whose head is this, and whose title?" They answered, "The emperor's." Then he said to them, "Give therefore to the emperor the things that are the emperor's, and to God the things that are God's."

MATTHEW 22:15–21

---

1. Epstein, "Sanhedrin," Folio 38a, line 31.

Then of the drop We created a blood clot,
then of the blood clot We created a lump of flesh,
then of the lump of flesh We created bones,
and We clothed the bones with flesh;
then We brought him into being as another creation.
Blessed is God, the best of the creators!

QURAN 23:14[2]

WORLDLY WISDOM—"IT ALL BELONGS TO CAESAR"

Our Ecological Crisis

IF THE LIFETIME OF Planet Earth were measured out on a timeline it would stretch down a country road for a mile and every inch would represent about 8,000 years. The existence of human life on this small blue-green marble would be represented only by the last inch of this timeline. Humanity has hardly lived here long enough to call the place "home." We've barely just moved in! Considering how long our host has been here and how much she has done for us already, it seems odd that only one day out of the 365 days in each year should be set aside as Earth Day.

As the end of the twentieth century approached, scientists began to worry about the condition of Planet Earth. What had for a long time seemed like pollution that we could eliminate, whenever we put our minds to it, suddenly presented itself as irreparable damage from which the earth and all living creatures might never recover. The air and water that supported all life would soon be unbreathable and undrinkable.

Of all the current crises we face today the survival of our planet is at the top of the list. Yet things still do not seem bad enough to us to change the way we live even when we believe what science is forecasting. We stick our heads in the sand and pretend it will all go away when someone else just figures out what to do.

In the meantime, we go on buying fresh fruits and vegetables already cleaned, peeled, and cut up for us on handy plastic trays wrapped in plastic. We continue to dump our waste into landfills and drive ozone-killing cars. We say to ourselves, "Someone will come up with a solution in time," or "It's all a hoax to scare us into spending more money," or "The Bible says the

---

2. Nasr, *Quran*, 852.

world will come to an end someday so why try to prevent it and go against God's will?"

Protestant theologians of the last century may have been skilled at articulating faith in the midst of various political crises but, along with most of us, they did not have a clear understanding of an impending ecological disaster. Most of us were led to understand nature as a submissive object at the disposal of its more creative subjects: human beings. Even for the most profound of our religious thinkers like Kierkegaard, Bultmann, Barth, and Niebuhr, nature and history were divorced and all that seemed to matter for humans was the making of history. Culture and history was what humans did *to* nature, to give it meaning and render it serviceable.

There are endless examples of the destruction that has resulted and continues daily from our attempts to dominate and use nature for our own convenience, comfort, and pleasure. Thousands of shocking articles are found on websites every day, e.g,

- crop failures in poorer countries lead to violence and upheavals.
- drought one year increases the risk that an African country will slip into civil war the next year.
- More than a third of the world's reefs have already been lost.
- Flooding river bottoms to grow hay means less water in the rivers for wild fish.
- Today forests cover only half of the area they did when the age of agriculture began.

Even though there are many people in the US who suffer from a lack of food, many suffer instead from the abundance of food available. We are the most overweight nation in the world. Nearly four million Americans weigh more than 300 pounds. Author Matthew Sleeth reminds us that, "Our appetite for meat, food out of season, and food from exotic places has a detrimental impact on the health of ourselves and the planet."[3]

Under our present political administration, many of the efforts being made by scientific and political leaders to change the way we are destroying the earth are being discontinued. The Environmental Protection Agency has lost funding, reduced staff dramatically, and watched as many of its regulations were overturned. Such federal expenditures did not seem "reasonable" to leaders who suddenly had the majority of votes and executive

---

3. Sleeth, *Gospel*, 140.

privilege, many of whom did not believe in any evidence of climate change and global warming to begin with.

We now live in a culture deeply divided over political issues, but the one issue that may soon make our planet uninhabitable is the most critical. We cannot afford to fight partisan battles over whether there is a crisis at hand when the scientific community agrees that if we don't do something to dramatically change the way we live our planet will soon no longer be able to support life.

Many will not live to see the full effect of this crisis first hand. It's easy for those people to convince themselves that they therefore have nothing to personally worry about. On the other hand, young people in Canada and the US are filing lawsuits against their governments for their legal rights to a safe climate and healthy atmosphere for their own and future generations.

Meanwhile, much of the "wisdom" of our nation's leadership today continues to assure us that the earth belongs to us to do with as we please, regardless of the consequences. Before his death in 2019, Frank Ackerman, one of the expert witnesses for the case, "Juliana v United States," answered the attorney for the Department of Justice when he asked, "What special training do economists have in ethical judgments?"

> What special training do any of us have in thinking about what other human beings are worth? Is that a matter for professional expertise? This is a question about what are future generations worth to us. The pure rate of time preference is a judgment about what you think future generations are worth.
>
> One climate scientist, who is also not trained in ethics, said the question is whether your granddaughter is less important than your daughter because she's born a generation later. And she said, they're both important, then the pure rate of time preference better be pretty close to zero. So I think that a problem like this that threatens lives and livelihoods and futures calls on all of us to make ethical judgments. This is not a matter of professional specialization . . . this is something we are all called on to do as human beings.[4]

---

4 Our Children's Trust, "Frank Ackerman.".

FOOLISH GRACE—"IT ALL BELONGS TO GOD"

Mark 12:13–17

> Then (some of the chief priests and scribes) sent to (Jesus) some Pharisees and some Herodians to trap (Jesus) in what he said. And they came and said to him, "Teacher, we know that you are sincere, and show deference to no one; for you do not regard people with partiality, but teach the way of God in accordance with truth. Is it lawful to pay taxes to the emperor, or not? Should we pay them, or should we not?" But knowing their hypocrisy, he said to them, "Why are you putting me to the test? Bring me a denarius and let me see it." And they brought one. Then he said to them, "Whose image is this and inscription?" They answered, "Caesar's." Jesus said to them, "Give to Caesar the things that are Caesar's, and to God the things that are God's." And they were utterly amazed at him.

In the year 6 CE the Roman occupiers of Judea imposed a census tax on the Judean people. Tax-revolts were common throughout the land during the time when Rabbi Jesus would have come to Jerusalem to celebrate the Passover Festival with his disciples. At Passover the people gathered by the thousands to remember how Yahweh delivered them from their Egyptian slave masters and led them to the land the LORD had promised to their ancestors; a land which they now saw ruled by Rome.

Pontius Pilate, the Roman appointed Governor of Judea, would have also come to Jerusalem for the Passover celebration. He would have marched in through a different gate, most likely, with legions of Roman soldiers ready to subdue any violence against Rome that might erupt among the throngs of Jewish pilgrims. In her biography of Pilate, author Ann Wroe describes Pilate as the emperor's chief soldier, chief magistrate, head of the judicial system, and above all, chief tax collector.[5]

The first century historian Josephus wrote of a time just before the ministry of Rabbi Jesus when Pilate erected statues of the Roman Emperor on a building adjacent to the Temple in Jerusalem. Jewish law forbade both the creation of graven images and especially the presence of such images within the holy city. Pilate was eventually forced to remove the statues to avoid a violent war with the Judeans. The political tension in Jerusalem is very high as this lesson from Rabbi Jesus unfolds.

---

5. Wroe, *Pontius Pilate*, 66–67.

Worldly Wisdom and Foolish Grace

The Jesus Seminar scholars voted this lesson into their red letter category which means that the majority of their scholars considered these words as being as authentically from Rabbi Jesus as can be determined. This red letter text is recorded in the Gospels of Matthew, Mark, and Luke and in non-canonical sources such as the Gospel of Thomas and the Egerton Gospel (the oldest known papyrus fragments of any gospel which dates to the first half of the second century CE).[6]

There is disagreement among the gospel writers about who came to Rabbi Jesus with the question about paying the Roman tax. Mark and Matthew report that it was "some of the Pharisees and some of the Herodians." (Mark 12:13, Matt 22:16) "Herodians" were a political group loyal to Herod the Great. Luke reports instead, that it was "spies from some of the chief priests and scribes." (Luke 20:20) The Gospel of Thomas, which lists 114 short sayings of Jesus, identifies the questioners only with the pronoun "they."[7]

From whom the question came doesn't matter much, in any case. There were always those who questioned a rabbi's teachings. Though "Pharisee" has become a pejorative term in our time, it is known that the Pharisees sought only a clearer teaching of Torah and that Rabbi Jesus was seen by this questioner as a "preacher in the tradition of the Pharisees."[8]

One interpretation of this story is that those who came to Rabbi Jesus with a question about taxes were hoping to get him into trouble because there was no safe answer for him to give. It is also possible that the question came from someone who hoped that Rabbi Jesus would support their fight against paying such taxes. And it's also possible that the question came from someone who was just confused about whether they should pay the tax or not. The question they asked was simple, "Is it lawful for us to pay taxes to the emperor, or not?" (Mark 12:14)

The synoptic gospels agree that this was the question Rabbi Jesus was asked. The Jesus Seminar translates this text, however, as "is it permissible?" instead of "lawful."[9] The question asks Rabbi Jesus to interpret Torah which was, in effect, interpreting God's will.

If Rabbi Jesus had answered their question with a simple "yes" or "no," he would likely have offended someone in the crowd. Those who were against the tax, and perhaps even part of a revolutionary group fighting the

---

6. Funk, *Five Gospels*, 103.
7. Meyer, *Secret Sayings*, 36.
8. Zaslow, *Roots*, 1.
9. Funk, *Five Gospels*, 102.

tax, might have turned against Rabbi Jesus if he sided with Rome and told them to pay the tax. And some of those people did turn against him. On the other hand, the Roman authorities might have arrested Rabbi Jesus for sedition if he had even hinted that they were not to pay the tax. This could have been why the Roman authorities decided to crucify him.

Rabbi Jesus responded as Judean teachers often did when they were asked a question: he asked another question in return. A common rabbinical joke asks, "Why does a Jew answer a question with a question? The answer: "Why not?" Rabbi Jesus used a pattern of debate common in first century CE Judea. When someone asked a challenging question, the one being questioned would respond with a counter question. By forcing the initial questioner to answer a counter question, the questioner's position often became more vulnerable. Their answer to the counter question might be used against them to reveal ulterior motives.

Rabbi Jesus responded to the question about paying taxes by asking his questioner to show him a coin. Then he asked the questioner to tell him whose image was on that coin. Most of the coins in circulation at the time were commissioned by the Emperor Tiberius and bore the image that Tiberius had chosen.

The Romans minted coins with 80 percent silver content which was not high enough to fulfill the 94 percent silver content prescribed in Torah for all temple coins. The priests were given permission to mint their own coins with 94 percent silver but only if they were engraved with an image of the Phoenician god Melquart whom the Romans worshiped. While not being happy that Rome required the image, the priests may have concluded that being allowed the prescribed silver content was more important than refusing the graven image. The moment the priests got the chance, which came during the first Jewish revolt in 66 CE, they started minting those coins without the image of Melquart.

While Emperor Augustus had issued hundreds of different coins, the current Emperor, Tiberius, had issued only three. Two of those were very rare but the third one, which Tiberius preferred, was quite common and was issued by his personal mint for twenty years.[10] Everyone knew that the coins minted by the emperors were blatant Roman propaganda used to remind the people that they were to serve and worship the emperor alone. Author Spencer Kennard writes, "For indoctrinating the peoples of the empire with the deity of the Emperor coins excelled all other media. They

---

10. Stauffer, *Christ and Caesars*, 124.

went everywhere and were handled by everyone. Their subtle symbolism pervaded every home."[11] We can only wonder if Rabbi Jesus suspected that it was this coin his questioners would have in their pockets. It wouldn't really have mattered, however, because the image on any of the coins in use would have been either Melquart or a Roman Emperor.

When his questioners had pulled out a coin and brought it to Rabbi Jesus, he asked them, "Whose image and inscription is this?" This question contains two powerful religious concepts which provided the scriptural basis that everyone expected from a rabbi.

Everyone knew the commandment handed down to Moses:

> You shall not make for yourself an idol, whether in the form of anything that is in heaven above, or that is on the earth beneath, or that is in the water under the earth. You shall not bow down to them or worship them; for I, the LORD your God, am a jealous God, . . . (Exod 20:4–5a)

To create an "image" representing a deity was considered idol worship in Torah. To make matters worse, Roman emperors declared themselves to be the son of a deity and were worshiped as divine beings by the Romans.

The concept of "inscription" played a major part in the daily Judean prayer called the Shema. The Shema is, to this day, often the first words of Torah that Jewish children learn to recite. (Deut 6:8–9) As Deuteronomy prescribes, the words of the Shema are to be "inscribed" on special paper, blessed by a rabbi, and enclosed within small boxes called "phylacteries" that traditional Jews wear on their foreheads and bind around their arms with leather straps before they pray. These words are also "inscribed" on small scrolls which are blessed and enclosed within hollow, decorative plaques called "mezuzahs" that hang on the doorposts of Jewish homes and synagogues.

It is said that on the Jewish high holy day of Rosh Hashanah three books of accounts are opened in the court of Yahweh within which the fate of the wicked, the righteous, and those of an intermediate class are recorded. Only the names of those who are counted as righteous are then immediately "inscribed" in the book of life and those people are sealed to "live." The idea of an inscription signified loyalty and faithfulness to the people.

> My child, do not forget my teaching, but let your heart keep my commandments; for length of days and years of life and abundant welfare they will give you. Do not let loyalty and faithfulness

---

11. Kennard, *Render*, 80.

It All Belongs To God

forsake you; bind them around your neck, write (inscribe) them on the tablet of your heart. So you will find favor and good repute in the sight of God and of people. (Prov 3:1–4)

The coins presented in this story to Rabbi Jesus may have born the "image" of the profiled head of Emperor Tiberius crowned with laurels representing victory and divinity. Around the profile of Tiberius would have been "inscribed" the words which translate, "Tiberius Caesar, Worshipful Son of the God." On the back of this coin would have been the Roman goddess of peace, called "Pax," and around her were the Latin words for "High Priest."[12]

Those who found Rabbi Jesus to be dangerous to their position and power may have used the Rabbi's words in this story as proof that he was involved in sedition against Rome. Luke records that, "... the whole assembly of them arose and brought (Jesus) before Pilate. They brought charges against him, saying, 'We found this man misleading our people; he opposes the payment of taxes to Caesar and maintains that he is the Messiah, a king.'" (Luke 23:1)

Rabbi Jesus' final answer to those who questioned him about paying taxes to Caesar was, "Give to Caesar the things that are Caesar's and to God the things that are God's." Everyone was amazed that he had answered the question in such a way that no one could find fault in what he said.

Did his answer mean that Rabbi Jesus supported the census tax of Emperor Tiberius? The coins may have been minted by Caesar but were the people being counted by the census tax created by Caesar? Did all currency, all the money in the Roman Empire, truly belong to the Emperor? While the Roman Emperor undoubtedly believed that everything belonged to him, the sons and daughters of Abraham believed that everything belonged to the one God; the Creator of all things. Rabbi Jesus' answer left them (and leaves us) no clear answer and much to consider.

Rabbi Jesus would probably not have supported violent revolt against Rome if he had truly taught the people to "turn the other cheek" and to "go an extra mile" when asked to carry the load of a Roman soldier. (Matt 5:39) Yet, since much of the Emperor's money was used to provide necessary infrastructure, like roads that led to healthy commerce, Rabbi Jesus might have supported some reasonable taxation even if the Emperor was cruel and oppressive.

---

12. Perkins, *New Interpreter's Bible*, 673.

Worldly Wisdom and Foolish Grace

This lesson from Rabbi Jesus may have had little to do with whether the people should pay taxes or not, and a lot to do with what belongs to Caesar and what belongs to God; a lot to do with whose image and what inscription we inscribe on our lives. Where do we place our ultimate loyalty and faithfulness?

The "Sanhedrin" was a group of rabbis that were chosen in each city to pass judgment on how the Torah should be interpreted. These interpretations were compiled into various documents called "Talmud" which interpreted religious law and culture. Talmud became an important piece of literature used in the Rabbinic Judaism of the early first century.

In the Talmud, the rabbis drew an analogy between the image that a human ruler puts upon his coins and the image that God puts upon the many "coins" of humankind (God's creation) saying, "When Caesar stamps his image on a coin, all the coins come out identical. When the One Who is beyond all rulers stamps the Divine Image on a coin each coin comes out unique."[13]

In other words, human being are created stamped with the image of the divine, but that does not mean they are identical, but that the image of God is unique, different in each individual ever created. We are uniquely and equally divine in nature.

This text about coins and images of the divine has much to teach about our understanding of our ecological crisis. If the image of the divine is on everything that was created by a divine Creator, force, or spirit, then the creation that humankind uses and misuses as if it belongs to them, must be understood as belonging to no one, other than a Creator.

Commenting on Elder Testament restrictions on the agricultural use of land, Matthew Sleeth writes,

> The land is not to be exhausted. It is not okay to get as much from every acre as a farmer or corporation possibly can. . . . God instructs the people not to harvest to the edge of their fields, not to pick up dropped fruit, and not to beat olive trees twice. Instead, the Hebrew people are to understand that long-term economic viability is not served by greed or the worship of efficiency.[14]

The Book of Exodus also presents what sounds like a Native American or Far Eastern concept of food consumption when it insists that one does not insult the animal one is eating by serving meat in the milk of its mother. (Exod 23:19) Compare this to modern practices of factory farming where

13. Epstein, "Sanhedrin," line 31.
14. Sleeth, *Gospel,* 141.

animals are fed the ground up remains of others of their species, or kept always out of daylight, or fed human estrogen to increase the fat in their meat.

There are probably no restrictions to "eat locally" in Torah. The Hebrew people could not have had any idea that food would someday be transported around the world to satisfy human appetites in huge machines that would eat up fuel resources and spread their poison into the air. Even though we cannot find biblical restrictions, we must realize that what we put into our mouths today matters not just for our own health, but for the health of our planet and for the life of multitudes of children and adults who die of hunger every day.

In 570 CE, The Prophet Muhammad was born in the Arab Middle East. Author Karen Armstrong writes,

> At the time of his birth, Persia and Bysantium were locked in a debilitating series of wars with one another that would fatally weaken both empires. Syria and Mesopotamia became a battleground, many of the trade routes were abandoned, and Meeca, his birthplace, took control of all the intermediary trade between north and south . . . As the sixth century drew to a close, the city was in the grip of a spiritual and moral crisis.[15]

The Prophet Muhammad would become the hoped for messenger of God called to speak the words of Allah directly to his people. He reminded the people that if Allah is the ultimate Creator imaginable, then what Allah creates has to be the best creation possible. All creation, created by the ultimate creator, is, therefore, inscribed as "the best creation possible." Islam teaches that the creation of the spirit that lives within human beings instills within humanity something divine, something that also bears the nature of the one Creator God, Allah. In the following quotation of Quran, the "We" refers to a "royal Creator."

> Then of the drop We created a blood clot,
> then of the blood clot We created a lump of flesh,
> then of the lump of flesh We created bones,
> and We clothed the bones with flesh;
> then We brought him into being as another creation.
> Blessed is God, the best of the creators!"
> Quran 23:14[16]

---

15. Armstrong, *Muhammad*, 22.
16 Nasr, *Quran*, 852.

National citizenship may, at times, include patriotism, voting, abiding by majority rule, paying taxes, and such, but such loyalty to country must always be measured against faithfulness to God's will and call upon our lives to seek justice and show compassion. There is a divine energy or will that calls all of creation to live in accordance with values that maintain wholeness, health, and justice as individuals and as communities.

All creation, every part of our land, water, air, plants, and living creatures are part of the "family" to which every human creature belongs. Even though English usually translates the ancient texts of Genesis to read that human beings were given "dominion over . . . every living thing that moved upon the earth," (Gen 2:28) the Hebrew word for "dominion over every living thing" is better translated as "given the roll of caretaker over every living thing."

Those who study the natural world are in agreement that we have misused and damaged earth's resources to a point almost beyond repair. Christians who read English translations of scripture as if they are the literal words of God claim that the destruction of the world is part of God's plan as recorded in the Book of Revelation. Yet the entire Bible clearly declares that God's plan is for wholeness, peace, and justice. God's plan is for a new earth, an earth full of people who live in the fullness of peace and compassion, not another planet that has simply replaced the first planet which we destroyed.

How would our relationships change within families, communities, and even nations if we recognized the mark of one Creator upon each human being and all of creation? Human nature may always react fearfully or seek vengeance for past wrongs or tempt us to consider creation ours to use for our convenience and pleasure, but if we are reminded that the Creator made and claims each created object, we might think twice about how we react to and treat each other and creation.

There is a holy scripture for Abraham's Tent, beyond the Torah, the Gospels, or the Quran; a scripture that was written long before the others and is referred to again and again in the all three texts. Creation itself is our earliest holy text. Creation itself is our first teacher about the Creator, self, and our relationships.

Human beings were created in the image of God, not so much because they were created with different abilities than the rest of creation or to have power over them, but because they were endowed with a distinct function as representatives of the Creator, who ruled over everything with compassion and grace and was to be worshipped over all.

It All Belongs To God

Since the beginning of time, humans have been quite comfortable with God's mandate to humans to "subdue the earth and have dominion over every living thing upon the earth." (Gen 1:28) It has felt natural to use the earth as we choose much like any human ruler would use the land over which they ruled. A better interpretation of "subdue," however, would be to "bring order out of chaos".

In Matthew's Gospel, when some in the crowd told Rabbi Jesus that his mother and brothers were standing outside wanting to speak to him, he said, "Who is my mother and who are my brothers? . . . Whoever does the will of my Father in heaven is my brother and sister and mother!" (Matt 12:48–50) Family was the ultimate loyalty in this culture as it still is in most cultures today. As the saying goes, "Blood is thicker than water!" Rabbi Jesus expanded the circle of family influence beyond anything we could ever imagine.

What if we were to believe that all creation fulfills the will of the Creator? Doesn't the apple seed only do the will of God, knowing how to burst open and grow into an apple tree? Is it not the will of the Creator that birds fly and build nests; that squirrels gather nuts for winter; that bears find a den and fall into hibernation as the snow falls; that glaciers carve out valleys; that leaves on the trees produce oxygen?

The Prophet Ezekiel wrote after the destruction of the temple in Jerusalem during the time in which he lived in exile in the lands of Jerusalem's captors. Ezekiel envisioned justice (the sign that the people were living in faithfulness to God's covenant) as the waters of a mighty river flowing from the temple of God; bringing life and health and healing to the people. (Ezek 47:1–12) If justice, including food, health, and healing, is established where the rivers flow, then we owe our way of life and every place we call home to God's creation of watersheds, rivers, streams, and oceans.

St. Francis considered all of creation his family. He called the sun and moon his brother and sister. Much later, John Wesley wrote,

> By acquainting ourselves with subjects in natural philosophy, we enter into a kind of association with nature's words, and unite in the general concert of her extensive choir. By thus acquainting and familiarizing ourselves with the words of nature, we become as it were a member of her family, a participant in her felicities; but while we remain ignorant, we are like strangers and sojourners in a foreign land, unknowing and unknown.[17]

---

17. Wesley, *Survey of Wisdom*, 8.

Worldly Wisdom and Foolish Grace

In 1990, thirty-four internationally renowned scientists led by Carl Sagan and Hans Bethe issued, "An Open Letter to the Religious Community" which held people of faith to a special accountability to protecting the earth.

> Problems of such magnitude and solutions demanding so broad a perspective must be recognized from the outset as having a *religious* as well as a scientific dimension. Mindful of our common responsibility, we scientists urgently appeal to the world religious community to commit, in word and deed, and as boldly as required, to preserve the environment of the Earth.[18]

All creation is looking to people of faith to lead the way out of this present darkness and the journey will not be easy. We must reform our biblical theologies, (a hotbed for the Church!). We have to rescue our cosmologies from the inadequate understanding of previous generations without placing unnecessary guilt on others and humbly embrace new truths. We have to renew our spiritual connections with the earth, with all organic and inorganic things, and redefine our own identity.

Most importantly, we must respond with prophetic voices and personal sacrifices on the behalf of people on earth whose voices we do not hear and others who may not yet care, and who may not yet believe, praying that those who have eyes to see, see, and those who have ears to hear, hear.

The Rev. Dr. William Creevey, Honorably Retired from First Presbyterian in Portland, Oregon, is a dear friend with whom I was privileged to work. Bill wrote about the holy text of creation. These are his words:

> We stand by holy places
> where continental plates have rumpled up rocky ranges
> and vast forests carpet the sweeping skirts of lofty volcanoes,
> where mosquitos bite and marmots whistle, and birds cry,
> where cascading streams tumble off ledges
> into canyons gorged by ancient rivers of melting ice,
> and ferns and flowers, gouging cracks in mossy walls,
> are mirrored on the surface of pool and pond.
> The dimensions broaden us.
> Beyond the distant curve of earth and sky,
> beyond the rising moon, constellations of stars,
> like silver dust across the night,
> mark the contours of our galaxy.
> There is no full understanding of the nature of the universe
> without a sense of grateful wonder.

18. Sagan, "Preserving."

It All Belongs To God

Though we plumb its depths and do our utmost to describe it,
the question of its meaning escapes us.
It is one thing to study the universe as subject matter,
to ponder its meaning in abstract prose,
another to listen to its song.
But when the heavens are singing in our hearts,
when our spirits rise to greet the morning,
stretching wings to wind and storm,
trailing mist and dancing on the sun-lit clouds,
then heart and mind encompass more of God
than any doctrine ever did.
Whether you believe or not,
whether you know or not,
life is telling the glory of God
as the firmament proclaims God's handiwork.[19]

---

19. Creevey, *We Stand By Holy Places*.

2

Children Will Lead Us

The wolf shall dwell with the lamb,
The leopard lie down with the kid;
The calf, the beast of prey, and the fatling together;
with a little boy to herd them.

ISAIAH 11:6[1]

People were bringing little children to him in order that he might touch them; and the disciples spoke sternly to them. But when Jesus saw this, he was indignant and said to them, "Let the little children come to me; do not stop them; for it is to such as these that the kingdom of God belongs. Truly I tell you, whoever does not receive the kingdom of God as a little child will never enter it." And he took them up in his arms, laid his hands on them, and blessed them.

MARK 10:13–16

The Prophet said, "Shall I tell you about the people of Paradise? They include every one of those who are powerless and slighted, yet who certainly fulfill any oath to God they make. Shall I tell you about the people of Hell? They include everyone who is violent, recalcitrant, and arrogant."[2]

1. Pelican, *Sacred*, 640.
2. Cleary, *Wisdom*, 46.

WORLDLY WISDOM—"CHILDREN SHOULD BE SEEN AND NOT HEARD"

Child Abuse and Gun Control

THE OLD SAYING "CHILDREN should be seen and not heard," may feel completely outdated to us, but we still live in a world which far too often treats children as fortunate or unfortunate acts of nature which become the property of their parents and whose responsibility it is to serve the needs of the family unit as much as their age and ability allows. Children come into the world requiring adults to provide for their physical care for years. Their caregivers often expect so much in return for providing for those needs, that they see themselves as entitled to rule over, to expect absolute obedience from, and to discipline those children even to the point of physical harm.

The viewpoint of this sort of parenting is often that children need to remain compliant, helpful, and dependent or their position as parent is threatened. Parents of teenagers know how their status in the eyes of their children can change practically overnight. Breaking the well-engrained patterns of strictest parenting, that assumes it knows what is best for the child, can be difficult, to say the least.

Our inability to see children as separate beings from their parents, with the same basic human rights as any other human being, has led to unhealthy relationships within families. It wasn't long ago, in the course of human history, that cultures even began to recognize and care about how children were treated. Behavior that clearly amounts to child abuse or maltreatment is still considered not only normal and appropriate in some cultures but even the parent's right to enforce as they choose. Such child abuse continues to rise every year and the US has one of the worst records of child abuse of any industrialized nation.

The statistics are shocking because so much more abuse goes unreported and we are still numb to the reality of much of the abuse around us. Children are abused and mistreated because they are not valued as highly as other human beings. Our lives may spin so out of control that we are unable to control out anger. We may self-medicate to dull our senses and hide from the things we can't face or control. We misuse alcohol, drugs, gambling, or many other forms of mind altering or distracting substances, in an effort to make ourselves feel better. When adults cannot handle the stress in their lives it is often those we trust the most and care the most about who receive the brunt of our anger; it is often the most vulnerable, the children around us, that suffer the most at the hands of adults whose lives are out of control. Children are the most available targets and the least likely to report such abuse.

The following data was reported by the US Department of Health and Human Services, and other agencies in 2018:

- The national rounded number of children who received a child protective services investigation response or alternative response increased 8.4 percent from 2014 (3,261,000) to 2018 (3,534,000).
- The number and rate of victims have fluctuated during the past 5 years. Comparing the national rounded number of victims from 2014 (675,000) to the national rounded number of victims in 2018 (678,000) shows an increase of 0.4 percent.
- For 2018, an estimated 1,770 children died of abuse and neglect at a rate of 2.39 per 100,000 children in the national population.[3]

The fact that we, as a culture, turn a blind eye to this epidemic of child abuse is evidence that we do not see the true value and wisdom inherent in children. At the age when human beings are the most creative and able to absorb information, (under the age of five years), we often treat children as if they are inferior, incapable, and little more than personal property.

The value of children is not demonstrated when they are demeaned, ridiculed, called names, physically hurt, frightened, or treated harshly. Parents and other adults caring for children are responsible for setting limits on the behavior of the children they care for, but they must also treat children as human beings deserving of compassion and respect. Setting limits and insuring that children cannot hurt themselves or others is necessary but must be maintained while inflicting no physical or emotional harm to the child.

"Spare the rod and spoil the child," is an dangerous myth that encourages some to believe that if you inflict physical pain on a child they will learn their lessons and will not become spoiled and disobedient. Hitting a child only teaches a child that it is allowable and expected for anyone to try to hurt other people. As a parenting technique, excessive physical discipline often leads to fearful and timid, violent and angry, or resentful children who struggle to build healthy relationships with others in their lives, including their earliest caregivers. Children abused in the name of discipline often grow up believing that they are bad, never good enough,

---

3. Miller, "Child Maltreatment," 4.

and deserving of abuse, or that the best way to deal with people or things you do not like is through physical violence.

Taking out one's frustration on others at the end of a difficult day is easy to do, but such behavior can often escalate, and will destroy relationships quickly. Many adults who were treated abusively as children have learned to treat children the same way that they were treated.

The devaluing of children is sometimes even couched in terms of how resilient children are. "They will bounce back," we say, as we try to convince ourselves and others not to feel guilty for unkind words or hurtful actions. Children can be more forgiving and understanding than adults at times, but this inborn gift of grace can also quickly be buried deeply within children if they are subjected to unkindness very often.

Children need to be accepted and loved by the adults and other children in their lives. It is a matter of their self-survival. Psychologically, children's self-worth is enabled largely by how they are treated by others. So, yes, children may give more second chances than adults, but those who are faced with bullying at school on a regular basis, or at home, will soon be damaged emotionally and in need of extensive therapy to regain trust in others. It is vitally important to treat children with kindness so that they do not learn to mistrust and abuse others.

The US reinforced the mindset that children are second class citizens when we separated children from their parents who were detained while trying to enter the US from Mexico at the direction of the Trump administration. Children were locked up in chain link cages as if they were animals with little need to be with people they trusted during frightening experiences. These young human beings were given little more than a thermal sheet to wrap around themselves. They were fed rationed food and denied health care, in many cases, until they became seriously ill. With little understanding of the English language, these human beings had no way to communicate and had no idea what had happened to the only people they knew and trusted.

The US administration had such little concern about these children that it took them weeks to hire a director for the Department of Homeland Security which oversees the work of the border patrols. They then continued to go from one acting director to another, with little progress on border reform as the number of children seeking asylum in the US continued to grow.

Judy Woodward of the PBS News Hour reported in 2019 that "New numbers reveal a record number of migrants apprehended (at the border) in fiscal year 2019. U.S. Customs and Border Protection says that the total was more than 850,000 migrants, more than double the year before. That number includes a record number of unaccompanied migrant children detained by U.S. border officials."[4]

I have become particularly aware of the issue of maltreatment of children while learning about the problem of child labor in India. I have traveled to south central India many times to work with an Indian nonprofit organization which serves the Dalit or Untouchable casteless people. I have witnessed how families in rural villages face increased hardships with crops which fail due to genetically modified seeds from international companies. These farmers sometimes migrate to the larger cities when their crops fail, to make money to support their families in the villages.

Farmers who are unable to make enough money to send back to their families often take their own lives in desperation. Sometimes parents are forced to sell their children to wealthy landowners for enough money, about $150, to buy seeds for another yearly crop. Unable to make enough on their harvest in any year to buy their children back, these children are forced into house or field labor for many years.

The children who are still at home spend their days helping their family in the fields. There is no education available to the children in these families who could not afford the required uniforms or supplies to attend school, even if their parents would agree to let them attend.

In urban centers throughout India, the children of millions of poor families are forced into prostitution alongside their mothers as fathers try to earn a living wage driving rickshaws, (the only allowable job for those from the Dalit/Untouchable Caste) or the children are also sold as indentured servants.

The NGO that I and many others from US churches have supported during the past 27 years, which is called the Bharati Integrated Rural Development Society (BIRDS), has continued to buy hundreds of children out of child labor for about $150 each. Many of these destitute children and youth have been sponsored so that they could live in boarding homes and attend the BIRDS subsidized school, both located on the BIRDS rural campus. BIRDS students often receive the highest marks of any other PreK-10th Class school in their entire region.

Think of the gifts communities around the world are missing out on because they turn their backs on their children. Children learn faster, are

---

4. Woodruff, "Behind the Record."

more creative, naturally friendlier, more inquisitive, and more trusting than most adults. Some communities see those attributes as blessings, while others feel these qualities make the children weak and of little worth. How long will it take us to understand that our children and youth possess the ability and possibility to inspire and lead our communities and nations with the clarity, honesty and kindness that we are unable to envision and offer?

FOOLISH GRACE—"CHILDREN WILL LEAD US."

Mark 10:13–16

> People were bringing little children to Jesus in order that he might touch them; and the disciples spoke sternly to them. But when Jesus saw this, he was indignant and said to them, "Let the little children come to me; do not stop them; for it is to such as these that the kingdom of God belongs. Truly I tell you, whoever does not receive the kingdom of God as a little child will never enter it." And he took them up in his arms, laid his hands on them, and blessed them.

Rabbi Jesus had been teaching, healing, and feeding crowds of people in Galilee for some time as his reputation continued to grow. Mark tells the fantastic story of Rabbi Jesus being transfigured before the eyes of three of his followers, Peter, James, and John, on a mountain top. It seems as if those three disciples had been given a special invitation to accompany their teacher to the mountain. The three were said to have even witnessed the prophets Elijah and Moses, who had died centuries earlier, talking with Rabbi Jesus. They later saw Rabbi Jesus covered and transfigured before them by a bright light.

When they came down from the mountain, Rabbi Jesus learned that the disciples he had left behind had been unable to "cast some demons" out of a young boy. Perhaps the disciples left behind felt that their teacher had picked his favorite students to go to the mountain. Perhaps they were feeling defensive for not being able to heal the boy, for they began arguing, later, about which of their groups of students was the greatest. Rabbi Jesus responded to their arguing by "sitting them down" and telling them that those who want to be first among them must be last; they must be the servant of the others and welcome those who are least and last, such as young children. (Mark 9:2–37)

Worldly Wisdom and Foolish Grace

The disciple John, still concerned about who was the greatest, said to Rabbi Jesus, "Teacher, we saw someone casting out demons in your name, and we tried to stop him because he was not following us." Rabbi Jesus said what amounted to, "So? What's the problem? Anyone who is casting out demons in my name is, in effect, with us!" Rabbi Jesus warned them not to put stumbling blocks before any of those little ones (poor souls) who believe in him, whether they are part of their "in-group" or not. (Mark 9:38–50)

Rabbi Jesus then left Galilee for the land of Judea where crowds gathered around him and he continued to teach. He was continually asked questions about Torah and would give his own Midrash understanding of the texts. This was the important work that his disciples expected him to be doing. (Mark 10: 1–12)

One day, the disciples tried to turn some parents away who were bringing their children to Jesus for healing or blessing. They may have been trying to protect Rabbi Jesus from what they understood to be the annoyance of desperate parents with ailing children. They may have been thinking something like, "We're in the middle of an important Midrash on Torah here! What are these people thinking, trying to push their grimy children close so that Rabbi might touch them? We can plan a time for him to do some healing later and they can come back then!"

The familiar image and words of Rabbi Jesus welcoming the children instead, draws us into a soothing, comfortable feeling of reassurance. Artists often paint this scene with freshly washed, blonde babies being bounced on Jesus' knee with big smiles on their faces.

Matthew and Luke retell this story almost verbatim from the Gospel of Mark: "Let the little children come to me; do not stop them; for it is to such as these that the Kingdom of God belongs." (Matt 19:14, Luke 18:16)

Matthew's only change is to use Kingdom of "Heaven" instead of Kingdom of "God." We mustn't start thinking about the afterlife here because the two phrases really meant the same thing, i.e., God's way and will for community. Earlier translations give us a better understanding of what Jesus meant by those words.

The early Greek text reads, "Let the little children to come to me and do not forbid them for of such is (*estin*) the Kingdom of God." The Greek phrase translated as "*of such*" is in the genitive construction which indicates the "composition" of the Kingdom. Actually, the Greek word for "is" (*estin*) also gives a sense of "consists of." [5]

---

[5] Scripture4All, "Greek Interliner."

Children Will Lead Us

The Peshita, an early Aramaic Bible translated into English, translated this phrase as, "Allow the little children to come to me and do not hinder them," (and here it sounds really strange, but it helps to read it literally), "because of those for who as these are, exists the Kingdom of God." The use of the Aramaic word "for" directly following the words "because of those" may simply re-emphasizes the word "because" (the two words can both mean "the reason why") or may mean the Kingdom exists "for" such as these in terms of the children being "for whom it is meant to exist." The Peshita helps us understand that this phrase could mean that the Kingdom consists "because" of children, or "for" children. [6]

Both the early Greek and Aramaic translations move away from the word "belong," which may have meant nearly the same thing as "exists" to some earlier English translators, but which tends to make modern readers think about right of possession or ownership.

A clearer translation of the Greek would be "for the Kingdom of God exists *because of* those who are like these children, *consists of* those who are like these children, and *is for* those who are like these children." This says more than, "Look at children and you are getting a glimpse of what the kingdom is like." If we use the Aramaic translation that the Kingdom exists *for* children such as these, we find another interesting interpretation. This translation could lead us to understand that the reason the Kingdom exists, in the first place, is *for* such as these who are vulnerable, naïve, trusting, and full of joy. Neither of these translations indicate that the Kingdom *belongs* to anyone exclusively.

A careful reading of this text also reminds us that the Kingdom exists in the here and now and not somewhere else in the future. This text is written using the present tense. The realm of God is not set apart from the present physical surroundings of earth. The Kingdom of God that Rabbi Jesus spoke of, the kingdom that he found revealed in Torah, is where we often least expect it: around and within those who are perceived to be without power or influence.

A biblical concordance lists few occurrences of the word "children" in the Elder Testament which present children in a positive light. In the Book of Proverbs, for instance, there are many lessons about *not* being like children, but none about *being* like children.

One text that does present children in a positive light in the Elder Testament is the prophecy from the Prophet Isaiah about the peaceable

---

6 Younan, "Peshitta."

Kingdom: "The wolf shall live with the lamb . . . and a little child shall lead them!" (Isa 11:6) The Tanakh, which translates its text from the original Hebrew, reads this as, "with a little boy to *herd* them."[7]

Edward Hicks, an early American Quaker preacher, who lived from 1820 to 1849, was also an artist whose paintings helped support his ministry. In one of his best known paintings, known as "The Peaceable Kingdom," you will notice that Hicks includes a scene of William Penn signing his famous treaty with the indigenous people of the land. This event took place centuries earlier, but may have reminded Hicks of the Peaceable Kingdom of scripture.

Hicks' painting of the "Peaceable Kingdom" represents the prophecy of Isaiah, found in Isaiah, Chapter 11, in which wild beasts, both prey and predator, will someday live together in one place in peace. One might think that a more powerful shepherd than a "little boy" would be needed to create such a peaceable kingdom, but this is what Isaiah predicted. In fact, the Israelites expected their Good Shepherd, their Messiah, to come as a mighty warrior who would rule with power and defeat their enemies.

When the prophet Isaiah spoke of his vision of the Kingdom, he spoke of the leadership and caregiving of a child. Perhaps it was the words of Isaiah that stuck with Rabbi Jesus. Perhaps the "little child" represented a kind of power for both Isaiah and Rabbi Jesus that was unlike the typical adult understanding of power found only in strength, wealth, knowledge, or influence.

We often think that a "child" is a symbol for those who are weak and vulnerable and that is certainly one way to describe children. In the case of Isaiah's text, it is a child that will lead and protect the entire kingdom. Likewise, perhaps some adults may be perceived as weak and vulnerable when, in fact, they may be capable of a different, but powerful sort of leadership and influence.

Mahatma Gandhi was a very small and often weak man. As he fasted to protest the unending conflicts between Muslims and Hindus in his country, he became very ill, even to the point of death. Even during Gandhi's most vulnerable days, his leadership and influence continued to lead his nation of diverse peoples toward peace and reconciliation.

The Prophet Muhammad lived during a time when idol worship had surfaced in Arabia. Arabs knew the stories and faith of Judaism and Christianity, the monotheistic religions of their neighbors. Some Jews and

---

7. Pelican, *Sacred,* 640.

Christians had lived in Arabia for a thousand years, fleeing to the east after the invasions of Palestine by Babylon and Rome. Some Arabs expected and hoped that an Arab prophet would one day revive the religion which began with Abraham, the religion and culture from which they had come as children of Ismael, Abraham's son with Hagar. Mohammad was among those seeking a solution to bring the people back to their ancestral roots and faith.[8]

Some Arabs had started following the faith of Judaism or Christian Jews, seeing the Jews and Christians not as separate religions but merely as different tribal associations. These traditional Jewish and Christian Jewish tribes worshipped as other Arab tribes did. Some Jewish or Christian Arabs even made Haj, a spiritual pilgrimage to the *Kaaba* in Mecca, alongside those who worshipped idols, which was allowed, at that time, within the holy shrine.

The *Kaaba* is the holiest site of Islam that sits in the center of the most important Islamic mosque in the city of Mecca. The *Kaaba* sits on the site of the original house of worship which is believed to have been built by Abraham and his son Ishmael. (Quran: Chapter 2, verse 127)[9] The ancient name for the city of Mecca was *Baca*.

Psalm 84:5–6 reads, "Happy are those whose strength is in you, in whose heart are the highways (pilgrimage) to Zion. As they go through the Valley of Baca, they make it a place of springs . . ." Many scholars believe that Abraham may have visited Hagar and Ishmael often in *Baca*.

Author Thomas Cleary, Ph.D. in East Asian Languages and Civilization from Harvard University, is the translator of over 50 volumes of Buddhist, Taoist, Confucian, and Islamic text from Sanskrit, Chinese, Japanese, Pali, and Arabic. In his book, *The Wisdom of the Prophet: Sayings of Muhammad, Selections from the Hadith,* Cleary presents translations of 224 authentic stories of the Prophet Mohammad, most of which come from the Hadith.

The Hadith recount the words and deeds of the prophet Mohammad himself, and are the basis of Sunna, or Prophetic Custom, which clarifies the teaching of the Quran in practical matters of inward and outward conduct. Included in Cleary's book of Hadith are words concerning what Christians refer to as the Kingdom of God:

> The Prophet Muhammad said, "Shall I tell you about the people of Paradise? They include every one of those who are powerless and

---

8. Armstrong, *Muhammad*, 30–33.
9. Nasr, *Quran*, 58.

slighted, yet who certainly fulfill any oath to God they make. Shall I tell you about the people of Hell? They include everyone who is violent, recalcitrant, and arrogant."[10]

Perhaps Mohammad had been imagining a child when he described the people of Paradise this way. Perhaps Mohammad was familiar with the tradition in which Rabbi Jesus had said that the Kingdom consists of those who are like children.

The Prophet is remembered as saying, "People whose hearts are like the hearts of birds will enter the garden of Paradise."[11] What a beautiful way to describe people who are like children, i.e., "people whose hearts are like the hearts of birds"! And how wonderful to be reminded by the Prophet that birds and other creatures also have a place in the garden of Paradise and the Peaceable Kingdom.

The Prophet was very fond of children and drew them to himself whenever he had the opportunity. He once said, "I stand for prayer wanting to prolong it, but then I hear the cry of a child, so I abridge the prayer, disliking inconveniencing its mother."[12] Clearly the spirit of children was felt and understood by the prophets of God who understood the will and way of divinity.

Professor Michael Jinkins of Austin Seminary explains how children are uniquely capable of tremendous accomplishments precisely because they are beginners, not experts:

> There is an art to becoming a beginner when you have been trained to be an expert. . . . The beginner, naïve perhaps, and untrained, is open to possibilities of understanding to which the expert, schooled in various technologies . . . can never again gain access.[13]

The Prophet Isaiah, Rabbi Jesus and The Prophet Muhammad must have envisioned the Kingdom when they looked at little children. There are many reasons why the image of a child might have created such visions for them.

One such reason is found in the story from John's Gospel of Jesus feeding the multitude. It is part of that story that we often overlook. In John's Gospel when Rabbi Jesus asked his disciples where they were going

---

10. Cleary, *Wisdom*, 46.
11. Cleary, *Wisdom*, 101.
12. Cleary, *Wisdom*, 117.
13. Jinkins, "Due Respect", 4.

to get bread to feed the large crowd, his disciple Andrew answers, "There is a young boy here who has five barley loaves and two fish, but what are they among so many people?" Jesus took the loaves and fish and distributed them among the people and all were satisfied. (John 6:9–11) Perhaps it was the generous gift of a child that made greater things possible.

In their classic book, *Learning By Heart: Teaching to Free the Creative Spirit*, Corita Kent and Jan Steward give a wonderful description of the behavior of young children:

> If you have a child of two or three, or can borrow one,
> let her give you beginning lessons in looking.
> It takes just a few minutes.
> Ask the child to come from the front of the house to the back
> and closely observe her small journey.
> It will be full of pauses, circling, touching and picking up
> in order to smell, shake, taste, rub, and scrape.
> The child's eyes won't leave the ground,
> and every piece of paper, every scrap,
> every object along the path will be a new discovery.
> It does not matter that this is all familiar territory –
> the same house, the same rug and chair.
> To the child, the journey of this particular day,
> with its special light and sound, has never been made before.
> So the child treats the situation with the open curiosity
> and attention it deserves.
> The child is quite right.[14]

There is much foolish grace to learn from this lesson:

- How we perceive matters of faith is important;
- Extend an open heart of welcome and compassion to everyone, even children;
- Do not judge who fits or doesn't fit in the Kingdom;
- Do not discount the ways of the inner child; and
- Respect all of creation, especially that which seems insignificant.

Even though we grow into adults with different skills and understandings, often it is a child, a trusting, open-hearted and open-armed child that will serve us best and lead us to building God's beloved community here on earth today or in the days to comes. It is the heart of the child, Rabbi Jesus

14. Kent, *Learning*, 14.

teaches, that reveals God's community and opens us to receiving, entering and living therein.

One thing that is universal about children is the curiosity that leads them to experiment, to try things out, curiosity that leads to what we adults would sometimes mistakenly call "mistakes." What does a loving parent do when things don't "turn out well," when their child "tries out" the world? Every adult who understands, forgives, teaches, and then sends the child out again to keep trying things out, perhaps with a few more lessons learned, will be a blessing for that child.

Perhaps the lesson about Rabbi Jesus and the children is not just about who *we* must be to enter the Kingdom but also about what God is like. Isaiah, Rabbi Jesus, and Mohammad had visions of the kingdom being filled with children. Perhaps God's beloved new community is to be a place where everyone is to be like children and where our efforts to get things right are understood, forgiven, and seen by the one divine Creator, as an opportunity to learn and try again.

3

Plant Seeds and Tend the Soil

For as the rain or snow drops from heaven,
And returns not there,
But soaks the earth
And makes it bring forth vegetation,
Yielding seed for sowing and bread for eating,
So is the word that issues from My mouth:
It does not come back to Me unfulfilled,
But performs what I purpose,
Achieve what I sent it to do.

Isaiah 55:10–11[1]

Listen! A sower went out to sow. And as he sowed, some seed fell on the path, and the birds came and ate it up. Other seed fell on rocky ground, where it did not have much soil, and it sprang up quickly, since it had no depth of soil. And when the sun rose, it was scorched; and since it had no root, it withered away. Other seed fell among thorns, and the thorns grew up and choked it, and it yielded no grain. Other seed fell into good soil and brought forth grain, growing up and increasing and yielding thirty and sixty and a hundred—fold.

Mark 4:3–9

---

1. Pelican, *Sacred*, 737.

The Prophet said, "The guidance and knowledge with which God has sent me are like abundant rain falling on the earth. Some of the earth is good soil that has absorbed the water and produces abundant grass and herbage. Some of it is hard ground that holds back the water so that God may benefit people thereby, as they use it for drinking, watering animals, and irrigating tillage. And some of the rain falls on another portion of earth that is only a lowland, which neither holds water nor produces herbage.

The first simile is that of one who understands the religion of God, who is benefited by what God has sent me with, and who learns and teaches. The last simile is that of one who does not raise his head for it, and does not accept the guidance of God, with which I have been sent."[2]

WORLDLY WISDOM—"YOU CAN'T CHANGE HUMAN NATURE"

Depravity of Human Nature

THERE HAS LONG BEEN a certain cynicism that believes that all people are basically selfish, self-centered, concerned first and foremost with their own pleasure, and that they cannot change such attitudes because they are simply part of being human. If human nature cannot be changed, some people take the viewpoint so far as to believe that they have every right to be that way.

Some folks are quick to blame any behavior that is less-than-admirable on the simple reality of "human nature." The argument is that because humans were created as mere mortals, rather than super heroes or mythical creatures with special powers, they must not be blamed for being anything other than weakly flawed human creatures.

Is there any such thing as "basic human nature?" Individuals are considered so unique today that thinking about any shared characteristics of the human species is rare. An article in "New Scientist" from 2012 includes some of the traits that all human beings seem to share. First of all, although many mammals play, "no other species (except the human) pursues such a wide variety of entertainment or spends so much time enjoying themselves . . . What sets us apart is the fact that we play with objects and with language. . . . Human play is imaginative."[3]

2. Cleary, *Wisdom*, 70–71.
3. Holmes, "Human Nature."

Plant Seeds and Tend the Soil

Humans are a unique species because they love science and are set apart by a drive to know "why" things happen. Humans have a much more elaborate system of rules, taboos, and etiquette than even our closest primate relatives. Human are unique in that they cook meals and therefore eat more calories with less chewing and gather at regular times to eat together. Humans are the only species which engages in sexual practices privately which anthropologists claim evolved because of a competition for females. Finally, Holmes and Douglas claim that though some animals are now thought to actual communicate with a form of "language" like humans, only humans have the compulsion to talk about other people, i.e. gossip.[4]

With these specifically human traits one can see that human nature has a lot to do with "control," whether it be through pleasing ourselves, understanding, setting rules, regulating food, competing, or gossip. The advanced consciousness of the human brain may have led us toward being *able* to control, and therefore *wanting* to control, more often.

Misleading interpretations of the story of "original sin" in the book of Genesis claim that, due to her weakness, Eve was tempted by the serpent to disobey God. Supposedly, both Eve and Adam were so weak in their humanity that they decided to eat the fruit from the tree of Knowledge of which God had commanded them not to eat. Weak and disobedient, their "sin" caused God to banish them from the Garden of Eden and all humanity was therefore cursed and made to struggle in a less than perfect world. (Gen 2:15–16; 3:1–14, 22–24)

Psychoanalyst Carl Jung referred to this depraved human nature as our "shadow" writing that, "When it appears . . . it is quite within the bounds of possibility for a man (sic) to recognize the relative evil of his nature, but it is a rare and shattering experience for him to gaze into the face of absolute evil."[5]

In Australia in 2011, The World Transformation Movement published a condensed version of Jeremy Griffith's earlier treatise "Freedom" which was entitled "The Book of Real Answers to Everything!" In this book, Griffith took on many of the questions which plagued humanity including: "Are humans good or are we possibly the terrible mistake that all the evidence seems to unequivocally indicate we might be?"[6]

---

4. Holmes, "Human Nature."
5. Jung, "Aion." Vol 9/2.
6. Griffith, *Real Answers*, 102.

Griffith began by claiming that "the biological theories of Social Darwinism, Evolutionary Psychology, (and the like) which argue that we are competitive and selfish because our genes themselves are competitive and selfish, can't be the *real* explanation for our behavior."[7]

Griffith claims that our genes can't be responsible for our bad behavior because 1) "our human behavior involves our unique and fully conscious thinking mind" and 2) "we humans have altruistic, cooperative, loving moral instincts—what we recognize as our 'conscience.'"[8] Griffith places the blame, instead, on our nervous system:

> Nerves were originally developed for the coordination of movement in animals but, once developed, their ability to store impressions—which is what we refer to as 'memory'—gave rise to the potential to develop understanding of cause and effect.... (Developed and refined over time), nerves (become able to) sufficiently associate information to reason how experiences are related, learn to understand and become conscious of... the relationship between events that occur through time... Our conscious intellect is then in a position to wrest control from our gene-based learning system's instincts which, up until then, had been controlling our lives...
>
> However, it is at this juncture, when our conscious intellect challenges our instincts for control, that a terrible battle breaks out between our instincts and intellect, the effect of which is the extremely competitive, selfish and aggressive state that we call the human condition.[9]

In other words, our instinctual genes begin to fight against our intellectually conscious nerves when it comes to figuring out how to manage life. "The conscious intellect fights back by attacking or denying the instinct's unjust criticism . . . and attempting to prove the instinct's unjust criticism wrong . . . and thus "the fully conscious mind—the psychologically upset, angry, alienated, and egocentric human–condition–afflicted state appeared."[10]

Griffith and the World Transformation Movement see this explanation of the human condition as "redeeming and rehabilitating." Though we

---

7. Griffith, *Real Answers*, 104.
8. Griffith, *Real Answers*, 104.
9. Griffith, *Real Answers*, 105.
10. Griffith, *Real Answers*, 106.

have been conscious beings for two million years, understanding the human condition may finally help us *heal* the human condition.[11]

Finally! Now we can give at least one scientific explanation of why we can release ourselves or others from blame by saying, "Don't be so hard on you! You're only human!" When compassion, forgiveness, understanding, patience, courage, generosity, humility, or any behavior asks too much from us, asks for a little more effort or maturity, or a little less self-centeredness, we can give the excuse that "our genes were fighting against our nerves" so our "human–condition–afflicted state appeared." This may even be seen as a kind and helpful response for not behaving better. Expecting ourselves or others to try harder seems cruel since we are "only human."

If human beings are weak creatures who cannot be expected to be any better person than they are, then why should we expect anything more from our efforts to change the world? If people can't be expected to exhibit better behavior because they are merely human, then it would seem impossible to change a group of people, a neighborhood, or an entire culture.

When it seems impossible to effect any change, people don't even try to do so. People are often convinced that the seeds of morality, ethics, or simple kindness are just going to fall on soil packed into cement by centuries of tradition, prejudice, and fear; that their seeds that are just going to be suffocated by the weeds of peer pressure, stereotyping, conspiracy theories, etc. or devoured by crows feasting on our wide-eyed innocence and Pollyanna perspectives.

The great failures of human societies continually discourage our attempts to hope that things could get better. This also makes it difficult to see things in perspective and celebrate the steps that many civilizations have taken toward justice throughout history. When the news media feels responsible to keep us informed of wrong doing and the disastrous consequences of human behavior and shares only snippets of honorable behavior in our communities, it's easy to feel very discouraged about making a difference at all.

---

11. Griffith, *Real Answers*, 106.

Worldly Wisdom and Foolish Grace

FOOLISH GRACE—"PLANT SEEDS AND TEND THE SOIL!"

Mark 4:3–9

> Listen! A sower went out to sow. And as he sowed, some seed fell on the path, and the birds came and ate it up. Other seed fell on rocky ground, where it did not have much soil, and it sprang up quickly, since it had no depth of soil. And when the sun rose, it was scorched; and since it had no root, it withered away. Other seed fell among thorns, and the thorns grew up and choked it, and it yielded no grain. Other seed fell into good soil and brought forth grain, growing up and increasing and yielding thirty and sixty and a hundred-fold.

Natives of Palestine say that it is time to sow the seeds when the thirst of the land is quenched. Palestine is a dry land with very little rainfall. Winter is the best growing season in the land not only because that is when rain finally quenches the earth, but also due to milder temperatures.

For thousands of years putting in a crop has remained very much the same for peasant farmers in the Middle East. The farmer starts off for his field early in the morning. His friends go with him as he has gone with them many times. Planting is a communal effort.

A small donkey is loaded up with a plow and bags of seeds and knowing the road to the field by heart, takes off down the path ahead of the farmers. The women and children follow along behind the men. When they reach, the field the men and women alike pull the bottom of the back of their skirts through their legs. They tuck the hem of the skirt into the front of their waste bands so that their skirts are not in the way and don't get soiled.

In the field, the sower, with a large sack of seeds tied over his shoulder, walks back and forth scattering seeds with both hands as evenly as possible over the small plot of ground. Following the sower, the donkey pulls the plow through the soil guided by the gentle directions of another helper. The plow gently turns the newly sown seeds into the ground.

If the seeds have been lucky enough to be turned into good soil and the rains continue, the seeds may spring up quickly and grow well. The parable from Rabbi Jesus about sowing seeds reminds us, however, that expecting all the seeds to fall into good soil can't be taken for granted.[12]

Each family's plot of land for farming is surrounded by a narrow walking path where the earth is firmly packed from years of foot traffic. As the

---

12. Grant, "People of Palestine." 133–34.

Plant Seeds and Tend the Soil

seed is scattered, some seeds inevitably land on the path where the donkey and the plow will not reach. Those seeds that are left behind on the surface become a quick and easy breakfast for the birds.

There is also the problem of too many rocks. The ground in most of the Middle East is covered with stones the size of your fist. It is a never-ending task for farmers to remove as many stones as possible. None-the-less, seeds are sown in fields where some hidden stones remain absorbing the warmth of the sun and drying up the precious moisture in the soil. Those seeds that do sprout will wither quickly from lack of moisture.

Thorns are a given in any field! Even in well-weeded fields, thorns and weed seeds float in on the wind or are dropped onto the fields in the digested food of birds. There is a continual battle being waged too see which seeds will sprout first and take over the field.

Fortunately, in the end, we are reminded by this lesson that some of the seeds, at least, will fall on good soil and grow to produce a crop for harvest. Sometimes the harvest may be unbelievably abundant in spite of all the hazards.

"A harvest of a hundred-fold" meant literally that for each measure of seed which was sowed, a hundred measures would be harvested. In Palestine the usual rate of increase was from thirty to a hundred-fold. A harvest of a hundred-fold was the most for which farmers could ever hope.

For Mark, this parable became a prime opportunity to give the early followers of Rabbi Jesus a word about spreading the good news of a loving God that Rabbi Jesus proclaimed. Rabbi Jesus, scholars suspect, felt that the power of a parable was lessened by attempting to explain it, but the author of Mark, can't help but add the explanation that the followers of Rabbi Jesus are like seeds sown by the sower every year.

Stretching the comparison to its limits, Mark adds that when these followers are planted in good soil they hear the word and grow into faithful believers. Leaving off Mark's interpretation and reading only the parable itself, we find that it teaches that as seeds are sown, some will die, some will grow a little, and some a lot.

The parables of Rabbi Jesus are thought to be among the most authenticly recorded words of Rabbi Jesus, as this was a literary genre often used by Judean teachers. The Greek *parabole* means literally "to throw alongside." Parables talk about one thing while referring to something else in the mind of the speaker that is thrown alongside, and remains unspoken. The problem with parables is to figure out what in the parable is being taught, "thrown alongside," without being spoken.

The parables of Rabbi Jesus typically turn common world views upside down. There is usually a certain twist of expectations in Rabbi Jesus' parables that leaves his audience scratching their heads. In this parable, the only surprise is that there does not seem to *be* a surprise. Instead of having some sort of paradigm shift, on the surface this parable seems quite logical, e.g., lots of seeds are sown and those seeds that are plowed into good soil grow best.

The folks that first heard these words from Rabbi Jesus may well have said to themselves, "Uh huh . . . so . . . is that it? We knew that already." Perhaps on the way home, though, some of them began to wonder about other metaphorical "seeds" in their lives and how they were sowing *those* seeds.

How do we sow "seeds" in our lives? Perhaps we have a conflict with someone at home or work or school and later on find ourselves thinking about all the nasty things that person has ever said or done; perhaps we think about how unjustly they always treat us; we may think about how we could get even by saying something equally unkind or setting them up for failure.

Instead of sowing seeds in the "good soil" of patience and tolerance for a harvest of greater understanding of the conflict, we let thorns of self-serving anger choke the potential growth; we let the hot, stony ground of pride and resentment scorch away life-giving possibilities. Just as a farmer is naturally careful about sowing their precious seeds, we must think about the soil in which we plant our "seeds."

Perhaps we're out socializing with friends and get into a conversation about what can or should be done to solve an issue someone has mentioned. We are full of great ideas. We have even read articles on the subject. We know exactly what needs to be done and how to do it.

Eventually, after our "good nights," are said, cars are driven home, and once home, perhaps with wallets a bit lighter and heads beginning to ache, we drop into bed. In the morning nothing will have changed and we will probably forget the evening's conversation entirely. Sometimes our good ideas and intentions get thrown about casually only to land on nothing more than a packed path where birds will feast.

"Good soil" for seeds is nourishing. It is able to firmly hold and protect the seed and yet yields gently giving room for the changes of sprouting and growth. "Good soil" for the seeds of our lives, is both loving and freeing; it is carefully and continuously cared for, watched over, weeded, and watered. The good soil into which we plant our seeds has heart in it, you could say; good soil is filled with "agape;" i.e., divine love, love that is an active verb rather than a feeling or emotional response, love that is sacrificial and unconditional.

Realistically, even when we sow seeds into the best soil, even when the words we use and actions we take come with the best of loving intentions, even when we sow our "seeds" as carefully as we can, some seeds will not come to harvest. Some of the "seeds" we sow will fall on packed soil or among thorns or wither from lack of moisture.

Likewise, some people will never embrace the words or ideas we share. Some of the first Christians were even killed by those who viewed their ideas about Rabbi Jesus as heretical. The history of religious persecution toward those of many faiths is long and violent. Speaking up for certain political and social viewpoints today can result in conflict, serious threats, and physical harm.

We can't always "preach to the choir." Words need to be spoken to those who may not agree with us. Speaking such words can be a very difficult step to take. We never know, however, when part of a message we share might have been heard in the midst of a group that seemed unreceptive at the time. Someone present, though silent for fear of repercussions, may slowly open their minds and hearts to the ideas they heard. There may have been some who disagreed completely with an idea at the time, but open up to it later because they had been given the opportunity to at least think about it.

The Prophet Isaiah lived 700 years before Rabbi Jesus. Many of his prophecies appear in the Elder Testament. Rabbi Jesus may have remembered Isaiah declaring the LORD's promise that just as rain from heaven causes seed to grow, the words of the LORD will achieve what the LORD intended them to do. (Isa 55:10–11)

In the first thirty nine chapters of Isaiah, God speaks to Isaiah of the "beloved vineyard" that has gone astray. God's anger rages against Judah, Israel, and the people of Ephraim and Samaria, yet God continues to ache for their people. God envisions a peaceable kingdom but foresees nation after nation waring against them. God promises to forgive and restore God's people when they turn back to following and listening to God alone. God's people were condemned, however, for idol worship, injustice and oppression against the poor, and for turning away from God. The people believed that God's anger led to their destruction.

Worldly Wisdom and Foolish Grace

Finally, in chapter forty, we hear the words of assurance from Isaiah that are typically read during the Season of Advent as Christians approach the Christmas Season.

> Comfort, O comfort my people, says your God. Speak tenderly to Jerusalem and cry to her that she has served her term, that her penalty is paid, that she has received from the LORD's hand double for all her sins. (Isa 40:1–2)

In the fifteen chapters of Isaiah that follow this well-known text, the tone remains reassuring. The everlasting promise of God will be restored and the people will sing a new song, for God is about to do a new thing. Many blessings are promised to Israel and Judah until finally, in chapter 55, the word of God invites everyone to enjoy the abundance of the land: "Ho, everyone who thirsts, come to the waters; and you that have no money, come, buy and eat." (Isa 55:1a)

Chapter fifty-five ends with the promise that "all the trees of the field shall clap their hands."(Isa 55:12) In the midst of this great vision of restoration and blessing, God speaks of the time when the God's very word will accomplish everything that God intends, as naturally as rain falls to earth and causes the seeds to grow.

> For as the rain or snow drops from heaven,
> And returns not there,
> But soaks the earth
> And makes it bring forth vegetation,
> Yielding seed for sowing and bread for eating,
> So is the word that issues from My mouth:
> It does not come back to Me unfulfilled,
> But performs what I purpose,
> Achieves what I sent it to do.
> Isa 55:10–11[13]

Can you imagine the beloved community that would exist if God's purpose for creation was finally complete and was trusted in the same way we trust rain to fall? This image stands at the pinnacle of everything good coming into being on earth.

But wait, then there are the first words of chapter 56, "Maintain justice and do what is right; for soon my salvation will come and my deliverance be revealed." (Isa 56:1) It is only *after* we create the beloved community and

---

13. Pelican, *Sacred,* 736.

understand every creature's worth in the Creator's eyes that we are then able to fulfil our calling to maintain justice and restore creation.

The Prophet Muhammad combines the images and words of both Isaiah and Rabbi Jesus:

> The Prophet said, "The guidance and knowledge with which God has sent me are like abundant rain falling on the earth. Some of the earth is good soil that has absorbed the water and produces abundant grass and herbage. Some of it is hard ground that holds back the water so that God may benefit people thereby, as they use it for drinking, watering animals, and irrigating tillage. And some of the rain falls on another portion of earth that is only a lowland, which neither holds water nor produces herbage."[14]

The Prophet sees God's guidance and knowledge falling upon him like abundant rain falling on the earth and, like the seeds of this parable from Rabbi Jesus, the Prophet understood that the rain falls on different types of soil, which he lists. Beginning with the good soil, the Prophet tells how the rain that falls on good soil produces abundant plants. The Prophet then envisions the rain that falls on hard ground that holds back the water, creating wells, lakes, and streams from which people and animals may drink and crops may be irrigated. Finally, some of the rain falls only on lowland, which neither holds the water nor grows any plants.

Similar to the interpretations of Mark following the parable of Rabbi Jesus, the Prophet Mohammad explains what he has told them:

> The first simile is that of one who understands the religion of God, who is benefited by what God has sent me with, and who learns and teaches. The last simile is that of one who does not raise his head for it, and does not accept the guidance of God, with which I have been sent.[15]

Muhammad explains that some people are like "good soil" because they learn from the word and pass on the benefits of the word that they have received by teaching others. Other people, however, are like soil that benefits no one, because they do not pay attention, listen, or accept the guidance of God.

Mark explained that the seeds are the word of God. The birds that quickly eat up the seeds sown on a packed path are the evil one who "eats

---

14. Cleary, *Wisdom*, 70–71.
15. Cleary, *Wisdom*, 71.

up" the word in those who hear it and whose hearts are hardened. The seeds that wither away in hot, rocky soil are those hearers who receive the word with joy but when trouble comes fall away from the message. The cares of the world and desires for wealth felt by other hearers, are the thorns and weeds that choke out the word. (Mark 4:10–20)

Rabbi Jesus may have told this parable not only to remind people to pay attention to where seeds fall, but to assure them that, in the end, they must never stop sowing seeds just because some of the seeds may not produce much of a benefit. Sometimes we do not get to see what has grown due to the planting of "seed, or rain, or word," but even if only a few seeds grow each season, the benefit will multiply.

Abraham's Tent teaches the foolish grace that we can trust that some of our seeds will grow, bear fruit and produce more seeds. In the same way, the rain and snow will continue to fall bringing life and giving water to all and the Word of God will endure for all who have ears to hear. We don't have to do it all ourselves; we don't have to change the world alone; we just have to keep sowing seeds and trusting the rain will come, so that some seeds will fall into the good soil of the heart or catch the wind and rain of the Spirit wherever it blows.

4

Love Fulfills the Law

The LORD said to Moses, . . . "You shall not wrong a stranger or oppress him, for you were strangers in the land of Egypt. You shall not ill-treat any widow or orphan. If you do mistreat them, I will heed their outcry as soon as they cry out to Me, and My anger shall blaze forth and I will put you to the sword, and your own wives shall become widows and your children orphans. If you lend money to My people, to the poor among you, do not act toward them as a creditor, exact no interest from them. If you take your neighbor's garment in pledge, you must return it to him before the sun sets; it is his only clothing, the sole covering for his skin. In what else shall he sleep? Therefore, I will pay heed, for I am compassionate."

EXO 22:20–26[1]

Now when the Pharisees and some of the scribes who had come from Jerusalem gathered around him, they noticed that some of his disciples were eating with defiled hands, that is, without washing them. (For the Pharisees, and all the Jews, do not eat unless they thoroughly wash their hands, thus observing the traditions of the elders; and they do not eat anything from the market unless they wash it; and there are also many other traditions that they observe, the washing of cups, pits, and bronze kettles.) So the Pharisees and the scribes asked him "Why do your disciples not live according to the tradition of the elders, but eat with defiled hands?" He said to them, "Isaiah prophesied rightly about you

---

1. Pelikan, *Sacred,* 119–20.

hypocrites, as it is written, 'This people honors me with their lips, but their hearts are far from me; in vain do they worship me, teaching human precepts as doctrines.' You abandon the commandment of God and hold to human traditions."

Then he said to them, "You have a fine way of rejecting the commandment of God in order to keep your tradition! For Moses said, 'Honor your father and your mother'; and, 'Whoever speaks evil of father or mother must surely die.' But you say that if anyone tells father or mother, 'Whatever support you might have had from me is Corban' (that is, an offering to God)—then you no longer permit doing anything for a father or mother, thus making void the word of God through your tradition that you have handed on. And you do many things like this."

Then he called the crowd again and said to them, "Listen to me, all of you, and understand: there is nothing outside a person that by going in can defile, but the things that come out are what defile."

MARK 7:1–15

And be virtuous toward parents and kinsfolk, toward orphans and the indigent, toward the neighbor who is of kin and the neighbor who is not of kin, toward the companion at your side and the traveler, and towards those whom your right hands possess.

QURAN 4:36B[2]

WORLDLY WISDOM—"THE LAW (THAT WORKS FOR ME) IS SUPREME"

Legalism and Immigration Reform

AS MORALITY AND ETHICS seem to have become relative only to personal desires in recent years, we in the US have found our culture dividing itself into areas of thought that continue to move farther and farther apart. We are a people divided. Still, one would assume that most people want to know that their understanding of morality is reasonable and mostly correct, so we continue to search for authorities to rely on and leaders to trust and guide us in the right direction.

2. Nasr, *Quran*, 209.

Love Fulfills the Law

Many people believe that strict conformity to the law of the land is the most important authority to follow in choosing how to behave, what to believe, or how to make decisions. Following the law of the land couldn't possibly be a bad choice, right? Most of us would like to think that laws are set by reasonable, educated, compassionate people with the best interest of others in mind.

Many of us have known individuals who live their lives legalistically. They may have learned as children from legalistic parents that laws were laws and that there was never a situation in which a law should be questioned. They might have even become "legalistic" about mere standards or suggestions that are made by public organizations, internet, professionals, etc.

Legalists will say there is only one right way to do something because somebody somewhere along the line declared it was the right thing to do. Legalists live within restrictive and nonflexible guidelines. When something happens that might make changing the rule necessary, legalists can become paralyzed.

Some people live as if they are "above" the law. Those behind the wheel of sports cars that zip in and out in traffic, ignoring the legal speed limit, those who park illegally and just ignore the mounds of tickets they receive, those minors who ask an older friend to buy their liquor, those who lie on applications, etc.

"Piety" is a state of mind in which one holds to a belief or point of view with unconventional reverence. Those who embrace legalism are often quite pious about their adherence to the law regardless of how that law is being applied or the circumstance involved. A pious person often expects to be respected or admired based entirely upon their strict following of a prescribed behavior.

It is safe to say that we don't all agree with every law all the time. Depending on how a law effects a personal situation, one may determine that law to be "fair" or "unfair." It is generally thought that trusted, competent people set up the US tax system full of laws and standards meant for the common good. Yet most people have felt, at one time or another, as if they didn't like paying one tax or another. When someone gets distracted and slowly eases above the speed limit, only to get pulled over for a ticket, they may not agree with that particular speeding laws or the judgment of that particular police officer. Laws are great as long as they don't restrict *me* too much.

It's not surprising that we've become pretty savvy at finding "loop-holes" where we can avoid the restrictions of a particular law. If the loop-hole itself is legal, then it seems reasonable to take advantage of a chance to get around the law, even though some loop-holes are less legal and less fair than others, and some are available only to the privileged few.

Some people blame others for laws that feel restrictive. The political party in control in Washington, DC is quick to pass the laws they feel will support their agenda and to blame the other party for laws that they think are holding the country back. It is very difficult to remain silent when laws are enforced that we feel are unjustly restrictive or are being applied discriminately toward specific groups of people. Many people conscientiously object to a law that they find unjust and oppressive.

US citizens have done a lot of taking sides lately based on some individual understandings of what is required legally and when and how laws are interpreted in light of human compassion and in the face of human suffering. The conflict over understanding and implementation of US immigration laws is a prime example of the potential abuse and injustice of legalistic thinking.

In the summer of 2018, thousands of children and youth from Mexico and Central America were taken away from their parents and families at the US border. Held indefinitely within fenced compounds because, according to leaders in Washington DC, their parents or guardians crossed the border illegally and the law gave the them no other option.

Eventually, the court systems ruled that the children had to be released into the custody of some responsible adult guardian. The law ruled that the children could not be held responsible for breaking immigration law. Tragically, there were many cases where no one could be found into whose care border officials were willing to release the children.

At the same time, hundreds of the adults arrested at the border were being held in government detention centers even though they were asking for protection from persecution and violence in their own countries. Some claimed that they broke the law by entering the US illegally. Others claimed they entered under international and US laws, traditional understandings of human rights policies that offered asylum for victims of persecution. What makes people see situations so differently?

Many Americans feel that the Trump Administration brought with it an atmosphere of legalism or at least the understanding that laws could be changed or interpreted to support the political viewpoints of those in power. When the law is used to the advantage of people who seek to protect their power and security rather than to protect the basic human rights of all people, the intent of that law is in jeopardy and legalism has distorted the value of the law.

The piety of those who distort and misuse our laws, traditions, or common human kindnesses, stands in the way of their becoming aware of and finding compassion for the needs of others. Such piety has always plagued community building, even during the time of Jesus when some religious leaders and their followers turned following the letter of the law, or finding loopholes, into a fine art.

FOOLISH GRACE—"LOVE FULFILLS THE LAW."

Mark 7:9–15

> Then (Rabbi Jesus) said to them, "You have a fine way of rejecting the commandment of God in order to keep your tradition! For Moses said, 'Honor your father and your mother' and 'Whoever speaks evil of father or mother must surely die.' But you say that if anyone tells father or mother, 'Whatever support you might have had from me is Corban' (that is, an offering to God) then you no longer permit doing anything for a father or mother, thus making void the word of God through your tradition that you have handed on. And you do many things like this." Then he called the crowd again and said to them, "Listen to me, all of you, and understand: there is nothing outside a person that by going in can defile, but the things that come out are what defile."

Most of the authentic sayings of Rabbi Jesus are "aphorisms"—short statements of a truth or opinion. The Jesus Seminar scholars believe that the most authentic words of this lesson from Rabbi Jesus are in the adage at the end, "It's not what goes in but what comes out that defiles."[3]

In this text, Rabbi Jesus is in the middle of a religious debate regarding the commandments handed down by Moses and the later practices and traditions that had arisen. Some of the Pharisees called these practices, "the tradition of the elders." The debate began when part of the crowd noticed that some of Rabbi Jesus' disciples had eaten without washing their hands first.

---

3. Funk, *Five Gospels*, 69.

Worldly Wisdom and Foolish Grace

An explanation is provided in Mark's text in parentheses. Such insertions are usually thought to have been inserted by a later editor, as they disrupt the natural flow of the narrative:

> (For the Pharisees, and all the Jews, do not eat unless they thoroughly wash their hands, thus observing the tradition of the elders; and they do not eat anything from the market unless they wash it; and there are also many other traditions that they observe, the washing of cups, pots, and bronze kettles.) (Mark 7:3–4)

It is likely that a later editor inserted these words to explain to non-Jewish readers what tradition was under discussion. Some translations add the word for "bed" to the list of things they wash. The original Greek has the word for "couch" also in the list and many English translations substitute the word "table" for "couch."

This parenthetical explanation is probably incorrect in claiming that the Pharisees, and *all* the Jews, followed these purity rules. According to Hebrew scholar Amy-Jill Levine, "it is more likely that the Sadducees and most other Jews did *not* actually follow this strict Pharisaic purity code very often."[4]

According to the Jesus Seminar scholars, the practice of washing hands before eating, washing food bought at the market, and washing pots, beds, etc. developed, over time, out of concern over infection. Moses had not passed down laws about such cleanliness but only the commandment of ritual bathing before entering the temple.[5]

The focus of the Pharisaic movement within Judaism at the time of Rabbi Jesus was to keep the faith and traditions of the Judean people alive within their ever-changing culture by encouraging the people to become more observant of their traditions and teachings. Never-the-less, as things changed within their religion and culture, their rituals were slowly adapted. It is unlikely that the Pharisees would have deliberately replaced the moral instructions of Moses with new ritualistic observances, but some reformation naturally came about as the culture evolved.[6]

Mark adds an example to these words from Rabbi Jesus reminding his readers of a tradition that was causing conflict in the community. It seems that the commandment to "Honor your mother and father" was being watered down by traditions that had developed over time.

---

4. Levine, *Misunderstood Jew*, 73.
5. Funk, *Five Gospels*, 68–69.
6. Levine, *Misunderstood Jew*, 73.

According to Exodus 30:15, devout Jews, male and female, rich or poor were expected to give a half shekel as a temple offering, or "corban," to God annually.[7] The Pharisees interpreted this law to allow that gifts of property and goods which were pledged to God did not have to be used to support aging parents. Gifts pledged to God were exempt, in other words, from the honor due to father and mother. This was part of an ongoing larger debate about whether the temple offering was perpetual, given only during the time of the "Meeting Tent," or given just once in a lifetime.

Often, if a person was unable to pay their "corban" all at once, they were allowed to pledge or promise this offering and pay it off a little at a time. There had been times when the tradition was to forgive these pledged offerings if families had other pressing needs. More recently the tradition was changing back again to holding people more firmly to their promises, tempting them to turn their backs on their responsibilities to their parents.

Mark claims that Rabbi Jesus strictly criticized those who defended such human precepts. According to the Peshita translation, Jesus criticized those who were defending this new tradition:

> Moses says "Honor your mother and father," but you say, "Should a man say to his father or his mother, 'My offering is what you have gained from me,' then you do not allow him to do anything for his father or for his mother and you despise the word of God because of the tradition that you have handed down."(Mark 7:10–13)[8]

The Peshita is the standard Bible version for churches in the Syriac tradition. Most biblical scholars believe that the Elder Testament books of the Peshita were translated into this version of Aramaic from the original Hebrew text probably in the 2nd century CE and that the Younger Testament of the Peshita was translated from the Greek. This Younger Testament Peshita had become a standard version by the early 5th century.

The phrase "My offering is what you have gained from me" (Mark 7:12) could have referred to an offering made to cover the parent's obligation to the temple or as an offering made in honor of the parent as the son or daughter's obligation. The offering, or pledge of offering, was now being claimed to somehow "benefit" the parent/s (as the Greek word is often translated) because the parent/s could now expect God to take care of them.

---

7. Hertz, *Pentateuch*, 68.

8 Younan, "Peshitta."

Worldly Wisdom and Foolish Grace

Rabbi Jesus goes on to say, "then you do not allow him to do anything for his father or for his mother." (Mark 7:14–15) If read literally this may sound as if the elders would then somehow stop the people from doing anything for their parents, but that would have been quite impossible either to expect or enforce. It is best to assume that this was a bit of exaggeration used to make a point and was said sarcastically. Mark or Rabbi Jesus may have upheld the injustice of this tradition, in effect, by saying that this was the same as not permitting them to do anything for their parents until their temple pledge was paid in full and thus effectively goes so far as to void the commandment of God.

Having corrected the people's understanding of corban, Rabbi Jesus returned to the original complaint about eating with dirty hands, saying, "Listen to me, all of you, and understand. There is nothing outside a person that by going in can defile; but the things that come out are what defile." (Mark 7:20) These words challenged customs that some were beginning to believe were sacred and that sounds, in the judgment of many biblical scholars, "just like Jesus!"[9]

The complaints raised by some of the Pharisees about Rabbi Jesus' disciples remind me of the criticisms about "those dirty hippies!" There were concerns raised in the 1960s and 1970s about the choice of clothing, lifestyle, and hygienic practices of some free-thinking, free-living, and usually younger people. Many had moved into communes or were choosing to live more simply. Some were not washing their clothes or bodies as often as "normal" people. Some wore strange hair styles such as dreadlocks.

Likewise, some of the Pharisees asked Rabbi Jesus why his disciples did not "walk" (as the word translates from the original Greek) in the tradition of the elders. They wanted to know why Rabbi Jesus' disciples did not follow the traditional customs of the people; why were they choosing to "walk" in the world in a manner that was different from other people?

Rabbi Jesus was disturbed by the attitude of those who criticized his followers and responded by calling the scribes and Pharisees "hypocrites." (Mark 7:7) He quoted the Prophet Isaiah (Isa 29:13–14) who declared that the LORD said, "the people honors me with their lips, but their hearts are far from me; in vain do they worship me, teaching human precepts as doctrines."

Years after the death of Rabbi Jesus, the Apostle Paul joined the followers of Rabbi Jesus. Paul's letters to small communities of the followers

---

9. Funk, *Five Gospels*, 69.

of The Way, as the teachings of Rabbi Jesus was first called, are some of our earliest and most authentic of all Christian writings. Yet, some of Paul's interpretations of Christ and Christ's message seem heavily influenced by the particular issues he faced.

To the followers in Rome, Paul writes about the role of civil law in the lives of Christians: "Let every person be subject to the governing authorities; for there is no authority except from God, and those authorities that exist have been instituted by God. Therefore whoever resists authority resists what God has appointed, and those who resist will incur judgment." (Rom 13: 1–2)

Some may choose to read this text legalistically, but if you read a little further, you will find a description of what fulfills the law:

> Owe no one anything, except to love one another; for the one who loves another has fulfilled the law. The commandments, "You shall not commit adultery; You shall not murder; You shall not steal; You shall not covet'; and any other commandment, are summed up in this word, 'Love your neighbor as yourself.' " Love does no wrong to a neighbor; therefore, love is the fulfilling of the law. (Rom 13:8–10)

The "letter of the law" is not necessarily the spirit of the law which allows the law to work for the common good. What "mere human precepts" do we consider to be doctrines within our religion and culture today? How might these contemporary human precepts distract us from concentrating on compassion? What "traditions of the elders" have become a part of the debates that divide our nation?

The priority of Rabbi Jesus was not those prescribed religious traditions which had melded into social customs. Sometimes those traditions were not bad in and of themselves. Keeping things clean while eating was, and still is, a good idea, for instance. This prevents a lot of disease. Likewise it was important to pay one's pledges to the temple. This helped the temple maintain its operation. Rabbi Jesus most likely followed many of those traditions himself.

The important matter for Rabbi Jesus, however, was how you lived in community; how you showed compassion to one another; how you took care of the people around you. Did those folks who complained about the "dirty hippies" ever stop to think about why those people embraced that lifestyle and what they were trying to promote or change—things like conserving resources, living closer to the land, eating healthier and more locally grown foods, ending warfare and violence and focusing instead on understanding, love and peace?

This is one of the clearest biblical texts to speak to the conflict over homosexuality. How is it that some folks can be so worried about who a person loves, who a person feels sexually attracted to, or who a person wishes to marry (things similar to, in other words, as what a person eats, what a person chooses from outside themselves) while not being concerned with unkind, disrespectful, manipulative, or hurtful actions that destroy human relationships everyday within married, heterosexual relationships?

It is easy for Christians, and others who have but a partial understanding of the law of Moses, to conclude that Judaism is centered on a strict systems of laws. While it is true that much of Torah records the instructions that were revealed to Moses on Mt. Sinai after the people escaped from slavery in Egypt, these instructions are based on the people's need for setting a structure that would ensure just and compassionate living.

Moses hands down the Ten Commandments at the beginning of Exodus chp 20. Exodus chp 21 begins with, "These are the ordinances that you shall set before them." Laws concerning slaves, violence, property, and restitution follow.

Exodus 22:21 begins to speak of the foundation of compassion and justice on which the other laws and ordinances are laid down. The foundation is that the people were once aliens in the land of Egypt. The redemption of the Hebrew people from slavery in Egypt is as central to the Jewish faith as the redemption that the followers of Rabbi Jesus experienced in his sacrificial death and perhaps we could even consider the Quran to have "saved" the people of Islam.

These acts of redemption are the foundation of many faiths which leads to loving neighbor as we have been loved. Rabbi Hertz writes that because we were once lost and afraid as strangers in a strange land, we are called never to wrong or oppress those who are now strangers in our land.

> This law of shielding the alien from all wrong is of vital significance in the history of religion. With it alone true Religion begins. The alien was to be protected, not because he was a member of one's family, clan, religious community, or people; but because he was a human being.[10]

---

10. Hertz, *Pentateuch*, 313.

Love Fulfills the Law

In other words, when we can see ourselves in those whom we most fear, those who are "strange" within our familiar surroundings, we can begin to see ourselves as creatures of the same Creator, first and foremost.

Rabbi Hertz talks of how often the Talmud calls for love:

> The Talmud mentions that the precept to love or not to oppress the stranger occurs thirty-six times in the Torah. The reason for this constantly-repeated exhortation is that those who have been downtrodden frequently prove to be the worst oppressors when they acquire power over anyone . . .
>
> Suddenly God throws these instructions back on us. If we, individually or corporately . . . afflict any widow or fatherless child, we will find that our wives become widows and our children fatherless. If the community, in other words, does not protect those preyed upon by individuals, the community is equally liable.[11]

The message from Allah found in the Quran 4:36b is similar:

> And be virtuous toward parents and kinsfolk, toward orphans and the indigent, toward the neighbor who is of kin and the neighbor who is not of kin, toward the companion at your side and the traveler, and towards those whom your right hands possess.[12]

The translation "virtuous behavior" comes from the Arabic *ihsan* which comes from the root for "beautiful" and denotes doing what is "beautiful and good." The "neighbor who is not of kin, or al-jar al-junab" means not only non-family members, but also those who are distant geographically or religiously. "Junab" is the Arabic word for anything that is distant, physically or metaphorically. "Those whom your right hands possess" refers to one's slaves and hints that slaves should be freed.[13]

Centuries later, Muslims envisioned the Prophet Muhammad being lifted onto the angel Gabriel's steed as they flew together through the night to Jerusalem and set down on the ancient site of Jerusalem's temple. There they were greeted by Abraham, Moses, and Jesus, and all the great prophets of the past, who welcomed Muhammad into their fellowship and invited him to preach to them. They called this his "night journey" or "isra."

---

11. Hertz, *Pentateuch*, 314.
12. Nasr, *Quran, 209.*
13. Nasr, *Quran, 209.*

Worldly Wisdom and Foolish Grace

Armstrong writes that during this night journey, the old tribal values Mohammad had held of heroism, prowess in battle, and ceaseless war against strangers, were changed:

> Instead of returning to his tribe, the prophet travelled far away from it to Jerusalem; instead of asserting his tribal identity with the arrogant chauvinism of jahiliyyah, Muhammad surrendered his ego; and instead of rejoicing in fighting and warfare, Muhammad's journey celebrated harmony, transcendence of the blood group, and integration with the rest of humanity.[14]

Human tradition is still used as an excuse, or at least a distraction, for not living compassionately. Thinking, "I wrote a check to charity this year so I have done my bit for the community" misses the spirit of the sacrificial love of Rabbi Jesus. Donating to charity is certainly a great thing to do. It's important that such work is supported, but how often does sending a check distract us from further, more demanding, acts of compassion?

It is active compassionate living that matters when it comes to building a more compassionate world. Listening to the compassion of the heart may not solve every moral dilemma, but it will lead us to seek higher ground, more important human values than those expectations and norms that our culture sets before us. If our thoughts and actions are based on compassion and justice, we will come much closer to faithful living.

Compassion is the compass that should direct our journey toward closer connections with the people in our communities, to listening not only with our ears but with our hearts, to stretching and working for greater understanding. The word "compassion" comes from two Latin words: *com* which means "to be with" and *pati* which means "to suffer." Compassion means to suffer with another person or to feel the suffering of another person.

Compassion is learned by "walking a mile in the moccasins" of others, as the old saying goes. Moccasins are not particularly efficient on rocky terrains. Every pointy rock or stick in the path can be clearly felt through the thin leather of moccasins. To walk in another's moccasins gives insight into their hardship and pain.

If we seek to feel compassion for others we need to begin by experiencing their needs, thoughts and feelings. Merely *feeling* compassion is pointless, however, unless we use our compassion to create justice and bring wholeness. When Rabbi Jesus taught his disciples to be compassionate it was always for the sake of helping others.

14. Armstrong, *Muhammad*, 85.

Love Fulfills the Law

In another parable from Rabbi Jesus, a father has compassion on his prodigal (wayward) son and that compassion leads him to throw his arms around his son's neck and kiss him, welcoming him home. Compassion leads the father to restore his son's relationship with the entire community. (Luke 15:20) Rabbi Jesus also told the people a parable in which a Samaritan (their mortal enemy) is moved with compassion when he finds a traveler beaten and left by the side of the road. The compassion of the Samaritan leads him to bandage the wounds and take the man to an inn for care. (Luke10:33) The story is told that Rabbi Jesus himself was moved with compassion when he came upon a funeral procession for the only son of a widow. With compassion he consoled the widow, touched the bier and restored the lifeless child. (Luke7:13)

The Epistle of James, written at about the same time as the Gospel of Mark, speaks of the importance of the "good works" of compassion:

> What good is it, my brothers and sisters, if you say you have faith but do not have works? Can faith save you? If a brother or sister is naked and lacks daily food, and one of you says to them, "Go in peace; keep warm and eat your fill," and yet you do not supply their bodily needs, what is the good of that? So faith itself, if it has no works, is dead. (Jas 2:14–17)

As Rabbi Jesus and others from Abraham's Tent taught, true compassion should draw us toward ending the suffering of others wherever it is found. Compassion that is put into action is the heart of the matter.

5

Season Passion With Compassion

Moses said further to Korah, "Hear me, sons of Levi. Is it not enough for you that the God of Israel has set you apart from the community of Israel and given you access to Him, to perform the duties of the Lord's Tabernacle and to minister to the community and serve them? Now that He has advanced you and all your fellow Levites with you, do you seek the priesthood too? Truly, it is against the Lord that you and all your company have banded together."

Numbers 16:8–11a[1]

"For everyone will be salted with fire. Salt is good; but if salt has lost its saltiness, how can you season it? Have salt in yourselves, and be at peace with one another."

Mark 9:49–50

The Prophet went out one day and prayed for the martyrs of the battle of Uhud. Then he went to the pulpit and said, "I am your vanguard, and I am your witness. And I, by God, I see my resource even now; and I have been given the keys of the treasuries of earth. And by God I do not fear for you that you will associate partners with God after my passing, but I fear for you that you will compete with each other here on earth."[2]

1. Pelikan, *Sacred*, 234.
2. Cleary, *Wisdom*, 3.

Season Passion With Compassion

WORLDLY WISDOM—"FIGHT FOR WHAT YOU BELIEVE"

Bipartisan Politics and Terrorism

Oxford's online "Learner's" dictionary defines "zeal" "(for/in something)" as "great energy or enthusiasm connected with something that you feel strongly about." It defines "zealot" as "a person who is extremely enthusiastic about something, especially religion or politics . . . fanatic."[3] We are often encouraged to "follow our passions" and to admire those who are most zealous about the causes they support. But sub-consciously, when we passionately hold onto ideals or defend *our* truth, we often experience the feeling of having power over others.

For example, political demonstrations became common before and during the Presidency of Donald Trump. The US presidential campaign of 2016 was filled with passionate people on both sides of the aisle. The campaigning, many thought, escalated out of control with slanderous language and the rush to fact-check everything that was said.

At the same time, demonstrations took place across the country for and against policies and perspectives of both sides on subjects ranging from immigration to foreign affairs to women's rights to health care. Many people felt more passion or zeal than ever for or against a certain issue and joined together to voice and demonstrate their concerns.

The right to "peaceably assemble" to express such concerns was continuously defended as our greatest constitutional freedom as US citizens. We have witnessed, however, that such gatherings can become less than peaceful when some of those gathered let their zealous ideals lead to destructive behavior. We can feel very powerful when we are in touch with what we are passionate about. When our passions are threatened we tend to defend them aggressively.

It doesn't seem too surprising to one side of the aisle to hear of those on the other side of the divide becoming militant as they express their passions, but when those on our own side suddenly join the anarchists, reacting violently against police and the "opposition", we may begin to wonder if there is ever going to be any resolution. We may have felt shocked that those who we felt were "right" also resorted to violent behaviors.

Many religious people are against abortions due to their beliefs about the sanctity of life and the commandment from God against killing. Many of us may allow each other the right to form our own opinions, but are

3 Oxford, "Learner's."

not so tolerant when passion and strong opinions encourage people to take matters into their own hands. Abortion clinics, patients, and staff have become the target of a few fanatics who decided that killing anyone in an abortion clinic is understandable and necessary.

Many of us are passionate about equality and justice. We would very likely step forward if we witnessed an individual being persecuted for their race, age, religion, sexual orientation, etc., but if our passion leads us to believe that we have the right to harm those who are harming others or destroying property, then we have allowed our passion to become a destructive force.

Freedom of speech, and the political cartoons and illustrations that enjoy this freedom, are another example of passion that gets out of control, fueling fires of conflict rather than strengthening the intended goal of persuasion. One such political cartoon showed President Trump with a knife to his throat and blood spewing from his nose and neck. The drawing went viral and resulted in death threats toward the artist, those who did not support Trump and Trump supporters. Trump's supporters feared that an assassination of Trump was being planned and began planning a counter resistance.

The freedom to peaceably assemble and the freedom of speech are being pushed to their limits these days as political passions run high among both conservatives and liberals. It is starting to feel like a return to feudal wars between opposing LORDs and their loyalists.

Standing up for ideals at all costs can ultimately lead to violence and terrorism. Before our own nation became the target of a terrorist attack on September 11, 2001, many Americans saw terrorism as something that happened only in countries far away. Today terrorism has brought a level of unprecedented fear and anxiety to school age children and youth, as well as those in mosques, churches, nightclubs, and even Walmarts.

Terrorism is defined as "the unlawful use of violence and intimidation, especially against civilians, in the pursuit of political aims."[4] "Psychology of Terrorism" by Randy Borum reports on the findings of 324 terrorism studies:

> An international panel of leading experts on terrorism met in Oslo to discuss root causes of terrorism. The purpose of this gathering was to provide inputs from the research community to a high-level conference on "Fighting Terrorism for Humanity" to be held in

---

4. Oxford, "Lexico."

New York on 22 September 2003.... A main accomplishment of the expert panel was to invalidate several widely held ideas about what causes terrorism. There was broad agreement that there is only a weak and indirect relationship between poverty and terrorism. At the individual level, terrorists are generally not drawn from the poorest segments of their societies. Typically, they are at average or over-average levels in terms of education and socio-economic background.

State sponsorship is not a root cause of terrorism. State sponsorship is clearly an enabling factor of terrorism, giving terrorist groups a far greater capacity and lethality than they would have had on their own.... Suicide terrorism is not caused by religion as such. Many suicide terrorists around the world are secular, or belong to other religions than Islam.... Terrorists are not insane or irrational actors. Symptoms of psychopathology are not common among terrorists. Neither do suicide terrorists, as individuals, possess the typical risk factors of suicide....

There are, however, a number of preconditions . . . for the emergence of various forms of terrorism: . . . Lack of democracy, civil liberties and the rule of law . . . Failed or weak states . . . Rapid modernization in the form of high economic growth . . . Extremist ideologies of a secular or religious nature . . . Historical antecedents of political violence, civil wars, revolutions, dictatorships or occupation . . . local or international powers (which) possess an overwhelming power compared to oppositional groups . . . Illegitimate or corrupt governments . . . Powerful external actors upholding illegitimate governments . . . Repression by foreign occupation or by colonial powers . . . The experience of discrimination on the basis of ethnic or religious origin . . . Failure or unwillingness by the state to integrate dissident groups or emerging social classes . . . The experience of social injustice . . . The presence of charismatic ideological leaders.[5]

We are quick to judge the "real" terrorism of extremists, yet it's also easy for all of us to find something within that long list of "preconditions" to which we can relate. We feel passionately about experiences of social injustice, repression, or discrimination. Any of us could come very close, at times, to reacting violently against such treatment.

Before, during, and following the impeachment hearings of President Trump, in early 2020, many of us sat on our couches and watched Democrats and Republicans get more and more passionate about what they

5. Borum, "Psychology of Terrorism."

believed to be the "truth". We were not really surprised that both parties were drawing deeper and deeper lines in the sand and that fewer felt they could ever cross those lines.

At first, the rhetoric was fairly civil; it didn't sound as bad as some British Parliament sessions I've tuned into! The impeachment trials in the House sounded fairly reasonable even though some of us probably tired of listening to the same arguments over and over again. The trial in the Senate also sounded repetitive, but tempers were contained and everyone behaved fairly well, except for perhaps a sarcastic tone here and there. The impeachment trials got harder and harder to listen to, all the same. *Our* "truth" got more and more "cemented" as we heard the reports again and again.

In the days that followed the Senate decision against impeachment, passions continued to escalate to a point that few expected. At the National Prayer Breakfast, the POTUS said he *disagreed* with a lesson Jesus taught—"Love Your Enemies." The news reported the firing of some witnesses from the House investigation by the POTUS. After his State of the Union address, Nancy Pelosi, the Speaker of the House, tore up her copy of the POTUS's speech.

The first State Primaries were being held at the same time as the State of the Union speech. The language of many candidates was different than during earlier campaigning. It began to sound like the candidates were picking up on an all-too-familiar crass style of bullying. Their comments became more passionate and more "cutting." The 2019–2020 political campaign has been a great example of how passion can turn everything to ashes.

FOOLISH GRACE—"SEASON PASSION WITH COMPASSION"

Mark 9:49–50

> For everything with fire will be vaporized and every sacrifice with salt will be seasoned. Salt is good; but if salt has lost its saltiness, how can you season it? Have salt in yourselves, and be in harmony with one another.[6]

Many people are passionate about backyard barbecuing and, if you are such a person, you probably know about the benefit of using kosher salt liberally on

---

6. Younan, "Peshitta."

large pieces of red meat that you have on the grill. Kosher salt does not melt like regular salt and will actually form a crust that will give the meat a wonderful flavor. We will return to this modern barbequing technique in a bit.

Although the saying found in Mark 9:49 about "salting with fire" is found in both Mark and the Q Source, neither the original form nor the context of this saying can be verified. Both Matthew and Luke adapt the saying into their gospel stories. The Jesus Seminar scholars concluded, however, that, "We are reasonably certain one salt saying goes back to Jesus."[7]

This is one of the most confusing texts in the Gospels, considering the variances in early Greek and Aramaic manuscripts, unless we understand the cultural context of temple sacrifice. There is general agreement between all the sources that Mark 9, verse 50 should read as, "Salt is good; but if salt has lost its saltiness, how can you season it? Have salt in yourselves, and be at peace with one another."

There are, on the other hand, at least a couple major variations of Mark 9, verse 49. The NRSV translation of verse 49 reads, "For everyone will be salted with fire." There is, however, a tiny footnote attached to verse 49 in the NRSV that reads, "Other ancient authorities either add or substitute 'and every sacrifice will be salted with salt.'"

The big difference between translations involves "the case of the missing second part" of verse 49: "and every sacrifice will be salted with salt." A biblical manuscript which is dated earlier is generally thought to be more original. Since the earliest manuscripts did not include part two of verse 49 we must assume it was added by a later editor, and the question then becomes, "Why was it added?"

The first part of the verse, "For every(one) will be salted with fire," leads us to ask, "How can a person be salted with fire?" The second, missing, part of verse 49, "and every sacrifice will be salted with salt," is less confusing. The second part may have been added to explain the first part, especially if the "and" is translated instead as "as," which is very possible.

The early Peshita Aramaic translation of verse 49 is different than the Greek translation. The Aramaic translates as, "For everything with fire will be *vaporized* or *destroyed* and every sacrifice with salt will be *seasoned*." The Aramaic changes being "salted with fire" to being "*vaporized* with fire" and changes "every sacrifice will be salted with salt" to "every sacrifice will be *seasoned* with salt."[8]

7. Funk, *Five Gospels*, 87.
8. Younan, "Peshita."

Worldly Wisdom and Foolish Grace

In Aramaic, the roots of the words "to season" and "to salt" are the same as the root for "to destroy, vaporize, or scatter." Depending on which prefix you attach to this root of the word, it is translated one way or the other. It is likely that there was some wordplay going on in the Aramaic text with words that sounded very similar but mean something a bit different.

"Salt" and "fire" are images strongly connected to the process of temple sacrifice in biblical times. This brings us back to the subject of barbecuing. Barbequing experts recommend coating meat with kosher salt before cooking because, while regular salt will make the meat taste too salty, kosher salt will form a tasty crust which will help evenly distribute the heat while flavoring the meat nicely.

Salt in the ancient world was essential and valuable because of its many uses. Most importantly, it could be used as a preservative for meat and it enhanced the flavor of foods. Salt diluted with water was also used to kill bacteria. Salt has been used, to this day, for soaking wounds or gargling to cure a sore throat. Grease fires can be extinguished with salt; putting salt on the barbeque coals will prevent flare-ups from the grease that drops off the meat. Perhaps ancient cooking fires were controlled with salt this way.

Salt was easily available for those who lived near the Mediterranean or Galilean Seas. Many others, however, did not have such easy access to salt water or time to gather their own supply. Although there is some disagreement whether Roman soldiers were paid their wages in salt or given wages specifically for purchasing salt, the words "salt" and "wage" have been connected ever since. The Latin word *salarium*, whose root *sal* means "salt," is translated as "salt salary, pension, or salary."[9]

Salt also played a major role in the Judean religion. A Salt Covenant is prescribed in Torah. Salt was used to seal covenants with God and with members of the community:

> (Moses commanded that) "every grain offering of yours, moreover, you shall season with salt, so that the salt of the covenant of your God shall not be lacking from your grain offering; with all your offerings you shall offer salt." (Lev 2:13)

> (The prophet Ezekiel declared), "You shall present (sacrifices) before the Lord, and the priests shall throw salt on them, and they shall offer them up as a burnt offering to the Lord." (Ezek 43:24)

---

9. Merriam, *Webster's Ninth*, 1037.

Season Passion With Compassion

In the book of Numbers it was commanded that the temple sacrifices be eaten by the priests as part of a sacred communal meal that maintained the holiness of the sacrifice. (Num 18:19) Archeologists have discovered sacrificial altars with the circumference of modern barbeques which include some sort of grate on which a sacrifice would have been placed. Oral tradition speaks of the long lines at the temple as many people came each day to make sacrifices.

If animal sacrifices were not salted they would have been more likely to be consumed by the fire, burned to ashes, or vaporized, leaving the priests nothing for their communal meal. The use of salt to prevent the offering from burning to ashes could have been a common technique used in all household meals that included meat cooked over an open fire.

We have often understood these verses on "salt" and "fire" to refer to being "tested" by or "tried" by God through various trials and tribulations, as in our being "refined in the fires" of life; or "seasoned" through our struggles. This metaphor is often used to refer to empowering faith that has become "bland" or "weak." We can remember, perhaps, trials in life that have led us to a renewed sense of strength against future trials.

In the passages that precede Mark 9:49 Rabbi Jesus warns the people not to "cause anyone to stumble," or, as the passages are often interpreted, "tempt anyone to sin." "Stumbling blocks" became part of a conversation Rabbi Jesus had with his followers when some were caught arguing passionately about who was the greatest and who should be allowed to perform exorcisms. Perhaps Rabbi Jesus was thinking that the disciples had been acting selfishly and excluding others, behaviors that could cause others to lose faith. Their passion and pride in following Jesus may have led to a misguided sense of loyalty, which led them to exclude others and see themselves as better than others. (Mark 9:42–48)

The Aramaic to English Peshita translation reads: "For everything with fire will be vaporized and every sacrifice with salt will be seasoned."[10] If it is fire that destroys, but salt that seasons, perhaps fire is a metaphor for passion and salt is a metaphor for compassion. "Passion" can become destructive when overheated and compassion could temper, or season, out-of-control passions.

It's an interesting coincidence that just as the two Aramaic words for "vaporize" and "season" have the same root, "passion" and "compassion" also have the same root word. Many people are passionate about those

---

10. Younan, "Peshita."

things that fill their lives with excitement and meaning. Unbridled passion can even be felt physically, sometimes, to the point of real discomfort. When unbridled passion is felt in anger against another person, our personal desires may over power us. Such passion can even be used as an excuse in courtrooms to lessen a conviction if the jury decides that passions can control our actions.

"Compassion," on the other hand, stands with and for another person; compassion focuses on another person; compassion sacrifices for another; compassion puts us in the shoes of another and puts the "other" first. We are much less likely to cause others to stumble when our focus is on showing compassionate toward others.

My paraphrase of Mark 9:49–50 may never make it into a biblical translation, but it deals with several of these complicated textual issues.

> The fire of unbridled passion will destroy everything, but everyone's perfect sacrifice for peace will be tempered with the salt of compassion. Compassion is good, but if the saltiness of your compassion becomes bland how will your compassion season your passion? Have the salt of compassion in yourselves and live in peace with one another.

Passion and compassion are wonderful gifts of life and both are necessary for experiencing life fully. Passion gives us motivation and energy to enjoy personal interests and talents, as well as the conviction to do the work of justice that needs to be done.

Our passions, however, always need to be tempered with compassion if we intend to follow the teachings of Abraham's Tent and live in peace. Rabbi Jesus had to remind his passionately zealous disciples not to let their zeal stand in the way of their love and the purpose and work to which *they* were called. In their zeal they had tried to stop someone from casting out a demon from a young child. (Mark 9:38–41) In their zeal they had tried to keep desperate parents and their ailing children from being healed by Rabbi Jesus. (Mark 9:33–37)

Torah tells the story of a man named Korah and his passion to serve the Lord. Korah, a Levite, and over 250 other specially chosen, respectable Israelite elders, came to Moses at Mt. Sinai one day challenging his authority. Korah, and those with him, said to Moses, "You have gone too far! All (in) the congregation are holy, every one of them, and the Lord is among them. So why then do you exalt yourselves above the assembly of the Lord?" (Num 16:3)

Moses fell on the ground in dismay and then said to them, "In the morning the LORD will choose who is holy and who will be allowed to approach him. . . . Each of you light an incense burner and lay incense in the burner and the man whom the LORD chooses, (the man whose incense burns first) shall be the holy one. You Levites have gone too far! (Num 16:4–7)

Then Moses said to Korah, "Hear now, you Levites! Is it too little for you that the God of Israel has separated you from the congregation of Israel, to allow you to approach him in order to perform the duties of the LORD's tabernacle, and to stand before the congregation and serve them? He has allowed you to approach him, and all your brother Levites with you; yet you seek the priesthood as well! (Num 16:8–10)

Korah and others with him were passionate about their faith and their religious order. They were so passionate, in fact, that they wanted to do more, to serve their God in greater ways, to be filled with the work of holy priesthood. Likewise, many today feel their faith in ways that drive them to greater ways to serve; many of the faithful are so filled with religious fervor that they dream of becoming missionaries converting lost souls. In past centuries some of that missionary fervor has been misdirected, leading some to mistreat, even to the point of death, those they sought to convert.

Korah and those who followed his leadership may have started out with the best of intentions, wanting to strengthen and support Moses, Aaron, and the other priests from the tribe of Levi in their work. As their passion became filled with more zeal it led them to feel jealous toward Moses and his priests. They began to imagine that Moses and the others saw themselves as greater than others because of their authority and privilege. They began to begrudge Moses and the priests of their positions. Their passion began to divide the community and create conflict. Relationships within and between families and others must have suddenly become strained.

The passion of Korah, and those with him, led them to forget the love their faith taught toward neighbor and strangers. Their passion to serve the LORD, through acts of love and compassion, became only a passion for power and authority over others.

The story of Korah ends with the punishment that Moses had prescribed from God for their unbridled passion. "The ground under them was split apart. The earth opened its mouth and swallowed them up, . . . So they, with all that belonged to them, went down alive into Sheol; the earth closed over them, and they perished from the midst of the assembly

(Num 16:33). Perhaps this is figurative language for a community that did not survive for long.

Author Cleary writes of the story of Muhammad's response to a battle in which many gave their lives for their faith:

> The Prophet went out one day and prayed for the martyrs of the battle of Uhud. Then he went to the pulpit and said, "I am your vanguard, and I am your witness. And I, by God, I see my resource even now; and I have been given the keys of the treasuries of earth. And by God I do not fear for you that you will associate partners with God after my passing, but I fear for you that you will compete with each other here on earth."[11]

Mohammad addresses his people after praying for the martyrs and assures them he is their biggest supporter. He is so proud of them that he will witness to the courage and valor of all who fought wherever he goes. He tells these soldiers that they are his most important and treasured resource for spreading God's message and encouraging others in the faith. He tells them that he has no doubt that even after his death they will all be faithful to Allah as the One God. He is about as confident and proud of his followers as he could possibly be, but there is *one* thing that he still worries about for their sake.

His *one* fear, the *one* thing that he is still not 100 percent sure of, is whether they will "compete with each other here on earth." The prophet knew the human condition well and knew that they would always feel the need to "out do" each other, that they would feel insecure in their worth if they were not seen as being as good as or better than other people.

It is human nature to compare ourselves with others, not only with those who are family and friends but also with total strangers. We strive and compete to do more and more, better and better, in our work, our accomplishments, our personal lives. Even in our accumulation of things we work harder and harder to own the right kind of car, house, vacation property, or investments.

Our drive to succeed can easily get out of hand. We forget to spend time with family, to pay attention to our health, renewal and healing. We forget to focus on enjoying the beautiful, good, and inspiring things around us. We forget to spend time noticing where and how we might help others in need.

---

11. Cleary, *Wisdom*, 3.

Season Passion With Compassion

The Prophet Mohammad understood how hard it was for his people to not compare themselves with others. Still today, we find it too easy to decide that we are either not good enough or too good in comparison to others. In either case, we are handicapped from being the person we were created to be. We cannot build God's new beloved community and treat others with compassion and justice, as long as we are comparing ourselves to everyone else.

The work for peace, justice and understanding deserves the best we have to offer. We are created as passionate, creative, strong-willed creatures for a reason. That is something to be celebrated! But we cannot let our human desires and emotions, our passions, distract us from focusing outside of ourselves and on the healing the world needs.

We are called to remember the sacrifices that the Judean people made to Yhwh both at the temple and in their lives. We must remember the compassion (salt) that kept their sacrifices whole enough to nourish their priests and to bring compassion to their neighbors. We are called to remember the sacrifices that the early disciples of Rabbi Jesus made in holding to his teachings of compassion even in the face of hatred and persecution. We must remember the concern of Mohammad that we do not let our passion drive us to "out-do" one another and thereby loose our goal of showing compassion. If we salt our passion with compassion our lives will be a perfect sacrificial offering to God that creates harmony with all creation.

6

Be a Good Neighbor

But Ruth replied, "Do not urge me to leave you, to turn back and not follow you. For wherever you go, I will go; wherever you lodge, I will lodge; your people shall be my people and your God my God. Where you die, I will die, and there I will be buried. Thus and more may the Lord do to me if anything but death parts me from you."

Ruth 1:16–17[1]

Jesus replied, "A man was going down from Jerusalem to Jericho, and fell into the hands of robbers, who stripped him, beat him, and went away, leaving him half dead. Now by chance a priest was going down that road; and when he saw him, he passed by on the other side. So likewise a Levite, when he came to the place and saw him, passed by on the other side.

But a Samaritan, while traveling, came near him; and when he saw him, he was moved with pity. He went to him and bandaged his wounds, having poured oil and wine on them. Then he put him on his own animal, brought him to an inn, and took care of him. The next day he took out two denarii, gave them to the innkeeper, and said, 'Take care of him; and when I come back, I will repay you whatever more you spend.' Which of these three, do you think was a neighbor to the man who fell into the hands of the robbers?"

Luke 10:30–36

1. Pelican, *Sacred*, 1420.

It is said of the Prophet Muhammad, that as a funeral procession passed in front of him one day, he stood up. When someone told him that it was just the bier of a Jew he turned and asked that person, "Is it not a soul?"[2]

WORLDLY WISDOM—"GOOD FENCES MAKE GOOD NEIGHBORS"

Our First Nation Neighbors and Neighbors who are House–less

"Worldly wisdom" puts forth mixed messages about who our neighbors are and how far our responsibility goes to help them. Most people feel that being a helpful neighbor, being a good neighbor, is the moral, ethical, and faithful thing to be.

High honors are given to people who rescue others from danger, sometimes risking their own lives to do so. These rescuers are crowned as heroes or heroines, yet these rescuers say things in response to such praise as, "Anyone would have done the same thing. I didn't even think about it. I just did what I felt I had to do."

We admire those in our community who volunteer their time and energy to serve those in need. Our children are raised (hopefully) to be helpful and caring to others. Many of us feel personally fulfilled when we are able to help others. Yet, we also hear a subtle message from society that encourages us not to feel guilty when we're not able or willing to help.

The Pacific Northwest is full of the pioneer spirit. Those early settlers on the east coast who chose to make the long trek into the western frontier developed strong feelings of independence and individualism. Those who survived the journey lived in harsh conditions in those wild lands and passed their strength and know-how on to their children. Their legacy is not entirely to be admired however, as some of the leaders of these settlers feared the indigenous people of the land, fought for power over them, and took their land by force. This led to centuries of retaliation and violence.

In 1493, Pope Alexander the VI issued a "Papal Bull" declaring that non-Christians should be forcibly converted by explorers of the new world and their land conquered:

> . . . any land not inhabited by Christians was available to be 'discovered,' claimed, and exploited by Christian rulers and (the Pope)

2. Cleary, *Wisdom*, 5.

declared that "the Catholic faith and the Christian religion be exalted and be everywhere increased and spread, that the health of (Christian) souls be cared for and that barbarous nations be overthrown and brought to the faith itself." This "Doctrine of Discovery" became the basis of all European claims in the Americas as well as the foundation for the United States' western expansion.[3]

Instead of treating the strangers that the settlers encountered in the New World with respect, instead of being good neighbors, we simply took control and sent them to places of "detention" called "reservations" where generations of tribal members have lived ever since. The pioneer spirit may have brought us far and enabled us to forge a new nation, but we let independent individualism convince us that you can't always be expected to take care of others.

We may join forces with generous neighbors to help those in need, as we used to do with community "barn raisings," but it is not considered selfish either, if we need to take care of our own needs first. Times can be hard and people often assume they're on their own.

Worldly wisdom says things like, "Good fences make good neighbors." Or, when faced with a situation we could help out with, worldly wisdom says, "Don't get involved! Just walk on by." A more logical excuse is, "You can't help others if you don't take care of yourself first, so you mustn't feel any guilt.

We have become a culture that values independence and every person being responsible only for themselves or their family. Is it any wonder that we have lost the desire or ability to see where needs exist, let alone to understand that we might actually help each other.

Professional caregivers advise taking care of ourselves first so we'll be able to take care of those who need our help. That is certainly true and important to remember. If we are sick, in the process of healing, or struggling with personal issues we may not have the energy to be very helpful to others. Taking care of "you and yours" all too often becomes an excuse not to recognize the needs of others, let alone help them. It might actually be the case that focusing on others, as we are able, could motivate and energize us to fix the things that need fixing in our own lives.

Aesop, the famous fable and storytelling slave of 620–564 BCE, is the earliest figure credited with the famous phrase, "Every man for himself"

---

3 Gilder, "Doctrine of Discovery."

Be a Good Neighbor

A great city was besieged, and its inhabitants were called together to consider the best means of protecting it from the enemy. A Bricklayer earnestly recommended bricks as affording the best material for an effective resistance. A Carpenter, with equal enthusiasm, proposed timber as a preferable method of defense. Upon which a Currier stood up and said, "Sirs, I differ from you altogether: there is no material for resistance equal to a covering of hides; and nothing so good as leather." Moral: *Every man for himself.*[4]

Aesop used the phrase to mean that everyone has their own perspective and understanding of what is best, dependent upon their own frame of reference, history, and background. That is hardly how we use the phrase today.

It is thought that the modern use of the phrase "every man for himself!" began with the British military as the specific command given when a situation had become hopeless and there was no other chance for survival. The order allowed individuals to surrender, flee, or continue fighting as they chose, depending on their individual circumstances. The commanding officers were no longer required, when this order was given, to provide supplies, medical help, or other support for their troops. The United States military does not currently use this order.

Today we use the phrase "every man (sic) for himself" to mean that every person is responsible only for taking care of their own needs and that no one is truly expected to help anyone else. Some might even go as far as to think, "Everybody's business is their own business. Who am I to butt in? People are proud and probably do not even want help."

Those thoughts are prevalent today because worldly wisdom has taught that we are not supposed to depend on each other, but to take care of ourselves. We have convinced each other that those who don't take care of themselves are irresponsible, weak, or lazy, and that we are "enabling" if we take care of things for them. If others try to help us, we feel guilty, refuse their help, claiming that "We're just fine, thank you!"

Those who have volunteered to serve meals to the hungry have often felt uncomfortable, at first, thinking that those who came for food must have felt uncomfortable. Week after week, however, these helpers come to see how grateful the diners are. The first time someone comes to receive a meal they may feel a bit shy, but those feelings pass quickly and are replaced only with gratitude for the time and energy volunteers give.

---

4 Fables, "The Three Tradesmen."

Worldly Wisdom and Foolish Grace

Some of our closest neighbors today may be "house-less." This term has come into use as we recognize what it is like to live on the streets. These "neighbors" do have "homes," places where they live sometimes with their families and close to friends, but they do not live in dwellings that we would typically call a "house." Often their "homes" are tents or shelters constructed from tarps and cardboard.

It is important to think of these neighbors as "people who *are* house-less," rather than "the house-less" or "the home-less." Homelessness is not the *identity* of a person but a *situation* in which that person, who is just like you or me, is presently living.

Those who are house-less may be the last people we would consider our neighbors. They are not like us, we think, and may be a threat to our homes and neighborhoods because of the trash they cannot dispose of properly. Some of "them" even have addictions or mental health issues. Certainly none of "us" have any of those issues!

We want municipal officials to take care of those who are house-less so that they do not have to live near us. We think things like, "Their situation is not our problem, but something paid leaders are responsible for. We pay property taxes, after all, so why can't that money go to "help" these people?"

Oregon and Portland especially, is known across the country as the best place to live if you are a person who is house-less. When asked why this is the case, one Portland citizen who was house-less told a reporter that Portland, and Oregon in general, treats people who are house-less better than most other places; our authorities are more understanding; there are more soup kitchens where you can get a hot meal; and there are more emergency shelters during extremely cold weather. I'm sure some Oregonians were dismayed to hear this news and thought immediately that the solution was not to be so generous or understanding. "It's all those soft-hearted liberals that are causing our house-less crisis!"

In most US suburbs today people no longer know even their closest neighbors. We no longer know when the people next door are in need of a tall ladder, a special tool, an extra set of hands, or a cup of sugar, let alone, when someone needs a ride to a doctor or clinic, or just needs someone to listen to the frustrations of their day. The most we connect with those who live nearby is to wave and say "Hi" from the safety of our automobiles.

How can we possibly feel any sort of compassion or responsibility for our neighbors who are sleeping on the sidewalks or in vacant lots if we see no need to help the people right next door? I'm sure that if a neighbor's house was on fire, or a tree fell on their house, or some other natural disaster took place visibly nearby, most of us would run quickly to see how we might help. Our natural instincts to try to help may take over, drawing out personal courage and sacrifice. But in normal circumstances, we think, "I've got enough to do just taking care of my own situation."

I once volunteered at a Neighborhood Emergency Team fair on a college campus near the church. The St. Mark congregation had volunteered to be the neighborhood staging area for emergency "first-responders" in the event of a massive earthquake. (One is long overdue to hit the west coast.)

A man whose property shares one of the borders of the college campus approached and asked me what he should do if the students from the college came over his fence and onto his property demanding some of the food or supplies he had saved for such an emergency. He feared that he and his family were going to be unable to protect themselves and their supplies from students nearby.

I stood there listening in disbelief. I finally was able to interrupt him long enough to let him know that the college already had train containers on site filled with more than enough food and supplies for their entire student body and staff. In my opinion, I told the man, he should feel lucky to have such a large and able-bodied work force close at hand that could dig him and his family out of the rubble of their home when the earthquake comes.

FOOLISH GRACE—"BE A GOOD NEIGHBOR"

Luke 10:30–36

> Jesus replied, "A man was going down from Jerusalem to Jericho, and fell into the hands of robbers, who stripped him, beat him, and went away, leaving him half dead. Now by chance a priest was going down that road; and when he saw him, he passed by on the other side. So likewise a Levite, when he came to the place and saw him, passed by on the other side.
> But a Samaritan, while traveling, came near him; and when he saw him, he was moved with pity. He went to him and bandaged his wounds, having poured oil and wine on them. Then he put him on his own animal, brought him to an inn, and took care of him. The next day he took out two denarii, gave them to the innkeeper, and said, 'Take care of him; and when I come back, I will repay

you whatever more you spend.' Which of these three, do you think was a neighbor to the man who fell into the hands of the robbers?"

The Jesus Seminar scholars consider this parable to be as authentically spoken by Rabbi Jesus as any text can be determined, calling it a ". . . classic example of the provocative public speech of Jesus, the Parabler."[5] Even so, the parable is found only in the Gospel of Luke where it seems to be added to a conversation, copied from the gospels of Mark and Matthew, in which Rabbi Jesus was questioned by a scribe or a lawyer regarding the greatest commandment and the road to eternal life.

Matthew follows Mark's lead and places these questions about the greatest commandment after Rabbi Jesus has entered Jerusalem to observe Passover. (Mark 12:28–34, Matt 22:34–40) While in Jerusalem, some of the authorities were constantly looking for a way to catch Rabbi Jesus blaspheming against Torah. (Mark 12:13)

In Luke the question about the greatest commandment is asked on the road to Jerusalem as part of what is called the "travel narrative." Rabbi Jesus has set his face toward Jerusalem and continues to teach his disciples and the crowds about the Kingdom of God. (Luke 9:51)

An almost identical question is asked in each of these accounts and Rabbi Jesus gives the same reply: "The greatest commandment is, 'You will love the LORD, your God, and your neighbor as yourself.'" It is likely that the oral tradition remembered Rabbi Jesus being asked this question often, and that he gave a similar answer each time. Each gospel writer, however, created their own context for the question and answer sequence.

Only Luke sets up a wonderful twist of narrative using a parable. When the lawyer in Luke hears Rabbi Jesus quote Moses (Deut 6:5) saying that he should "love his neighbor with all his heart, soul, strength, and mind," he wants to justify himself," so he asks, "And *who* is my neighbor?" In return, Rabbi Jesus tells him and those nearby the "Parable of the Good Samaritan" and then turns to the lawyer and asks, "Which of these three do you think was a neighbor *to* the man who fell into the hands of robbers?"(Luke 10:29)

Sermons and commentaries have long proclaimed that the lawyer asked the wrong question: "Who is my neighbor?" The right question, the question which Rabbi Jesus hoped people would ask, was, "How can I *be* a neighbor?" In other words, most of us have been told that the message of this parable is to stop trying to decide *who* your neighbor is and just start helping as a good neighbor should!

5. Funk. *Five Gospels*, 324.

Assuming that the original context in which this parable was taught is not known, we should read the parable separate from any context at all. "Neighborliness" does not even come to mind if we don't include the quote from Moses or question from Jesus about neighbors.

Instead, reading this parable void of any context, we must think only about what we would do if we found ourselves beaten up, laying in a ditch, and, more specifically, found ourselves being given aid by someone we saw as our "enemy." In this case, it is probably the one in the ditch that we are likely to relate to.

There is another story about Samaritans in Second Chronicles of the Elder Testament, a story that Rabbi Jesus probably knew well. Though temporarily united under King David and King Solomon, at the death of Solomon, Israel was split into two kingdoms: the northern kingdom of Israel with its capital in Samaria, and the southern kingdom of Judah with its capital in Jerusalem.

The Samaritans, those who lived in and around Samaria, claimed that they were the true Israel, descendants of the "lost tribes" captured and taken into Assyrian captivity. Both kingdoms claimed that their temple and their version of Torah were the most original and authentic. Both Judean and Samaritan leaders taught that it was wrong to have any contact with people from the other kingdom and neither was to enter each other's territory.

The Samaritans hated Ahaz, the king of Judah, because he had returned to worshiping idols and offering human sacrifices. The king of Samaria, Aram, eventually attacked the southern kingdom, killing 120,000 Judeans. Capturing 200,000 more of their ancient kinsmen, women, and children, they marched them back toward Samaria.

As they approached the capital in Samaria, the Prophet Oded met them and told them that even though God had delivered Judah over to them, God was not pleased with their rage and violence. Oded said that they were offending God even further by bringing the captives back to become their slaves and declared that the Judeans be released to return to their homes in Judah.

The Samaritan soldiers released their captives, clothed them and gave them shoes, food and drink and (listen carefully) they then anointed them with oil and provided donkeys for all who were too weak to walk and brought them to Jericho, back to their homeland. (2 Chr 28:1–15)

When Rabbi Jesus told this parable it is quite possible he was remembering the story about the captive Judeans who were cared for by

Samaritans; a story in which their ancient enemies treated them with compassion; a story about God's anger being kindled against those whose unbridled passion led to violence, regardless of what faith they followed.

As with Rabbi Jesus' lesson on salt and fire (see Chapter 5), perhaps it was the salt of compassion that Rabbi Jesus found in an enemy of his people; the compassion that seasoned the passion of old hatreds and retaliation and allowed the Samaritan to feel compassion for the person suffering in the ditch.

Author John Dominic Crossan reminds us of the enmity between Jews and Samaritans.

> If Jesus had wanted to teach love of neighbor in distress, any standard folkloric threesome would have sufficed. . . . If he had wanted to add a jibe against the clerical circles of Jerusalem, the third traveler could have been a Jewish lay-person. . . . If he had wanted to inculcate love of one's enemies, it would have been radical enough to have a Jewish person stop and assist a Samaritan. The literal point of (this) story challenges the hearer to put together two impossible and contradictory words for the same person: Samaritan and neighbor . . . and when Good and Bad become, respectively, Bad and Good, a world is challenged.[6]

Being a "Good Samaritan" is a phrase understood by both the religious and non-religious today. Most Christians know the parable behind this label so well that they assume there is little left to learn from it. Not many of us would drive on by if we saw someone lying by the side of the road, half-dead. At least that is what we'd like to think we would do. If we couldn't stop, we'd like to think that we would at least call 911 and be sure someone else took care of the problem.

The only issue we have today with this lesson from Rabbi Jesus is that it does not take into consideration how complicated situations like this can be in today's modern world. If we stop along a busy highway, we could be putting ourselves and our passengers in danger of being hit by a passing vehicle. If we give medical care and our care turns out to be inadequate, we could be sued. Still, all in all, we would like to think that we too would be Good Samaritans.

In December of 1970, 40 Princeton Seminary students participated in what they were told was "a study of the vocational careers of seminary

---

6. Crossan. *In Parables*, 62.

students."⁷ Though each of them had completed a brief questionnaire about being in seminary, as they arrived each was told that additional information would be gathered through a brief recording of their thoughts to be done in a nearby studio. Half of the students were told that they were to talk about what jobs seminarians would enjoy most and in which jobs seminarians would be most "effective." The other half of the students were told they were to reflect on the Parable of the Good Samaritan. Each of the groups had a brief paragraph to read, the latter being given the biblical text to read.

Then everyone in both of the initial groups were given either "high-hurry," "intermediate-hurry" or "low-hurry" conditions in which to leave for the other building and they were each given the same specific map and directions on how to get to the right door where an assistant would be waiting.

As each student walked to the other building, one at a time, they went down an alley where a victim was staged, "slumped in a doorway, head down, eyes closed, not moving. As the subject went by, the victim coughed twice and groaned once, keeping his head down. If the seminary student subject stopped and asked if something was wrong or offered to help, the victim, startled and somewhat groggy, said, 'Oh, thank you (cough) . . . No, it's all right, (pause) I've got this respiratory condition (cough) . . . Thanks very much for stopping though (smiling weakly).'"⁸

The results drawn from this study were quite interesting. The study showed that "subjects in a hurry were likely to offer less help than were subjects not in a hurry. Whether the subject was going to give a speech on the parable of the Good Samaritan or on the jobs seminarians preferred did not significantly affect helping behavior. In this analysis . . . of the forty subjects, 16 (40%) offered some sort of help." ⁹ Darley commented, "The frequently cited explanation that ethics becomes a luxury as the speed of our daily lives increases is at least an accurate description."¹⁰

This study has been the topic of many theological reflections, but few seem to mention an aspect of the study that is perhaps the most relevant to what Rabbi Jesus was trying to teach when he told the parable. The study also measured the "religiosity" of each of their seminarian subjects and divided the seminarians into distinct ways or levels of being religious.

7. Darley, "From Jerusalem," 103.
8. Darley, "From Jerusalem," 104.
9. Darley, "From Jerusalem," 104.
10. Darley, "From Jerusalem," 107.

Worldly Wisdom and Foolish Grace

While religiosity as an *end* did not affect the degree of helping in the first place, religiosity as a *quest* did affect an offering of *less* help but a different *sort* of help. Another category of *how* the subject tried to help the victim was added at the suggestion of the victim after his observation of the subjects.

> One style of helping that emerged in this experiment was directed toward the presumed underlying needs of the victim and was little modified by the victim's comments about his own needs. In contrast, another style was more tentative and seemed more responsive to the victim's statement of his need.
>
> The former kind of helping was likely to be displayed by subjects who expressed strong doctrinal orthodoxy. Conversely, this fixed kind of helping was unlikely among subjects high on the "religion as quest" dimension. These latter subjects, who conceived their religion as involving an ongoing search for meaning in their personal and social world, seemed more responsive to the victim's immediate need and more open to the victim's definitions of his own needs.[11]

The Samaritan (as opposed to "seminarian") is the crux of the matter in this lesson from Rabbi Jesus. *Crux* is Latin for "cross." The phrase "crux of the matter" comes from references to the cross of Rabbi Jesus. What better way to describe the Samaritan!

As Rabbi Jesus spoke this parable, his audience would likely have assumed that the person attacked on the road from Jerusalem to Jericho was a Judean like them. As potential rescuers came down the road, one at a time, listeners would have recognized a common three-part formula, something like in the story of the Three Little Pigs, in which the third little pig is always the hero.

First, a priest passes by, then, a temple worker from the tribe of Levi passes by, two characters who could easily have been preoccupied with their busy schedules running to and from the temple. The original audience may have assumed that the third person to come down the road would be a righteous Judean lay person, a fellow commoner like themselves, rather than some "holy guy" with his mind on other things like their "religious rules." After all, priests and other religious leaders were indeed commanded *not* to touch anyone who could be ill for fear of becoming ritually unclean.

---

11. Darley, "From Jerusalem," 106–7.

The third example, however, the one who was supposed to be the hero, turns out to be a Samaritan and the people suddenly lose their way in the story. Just hearing the word "Samaritan" would have made their blood boil. The instructions of their religious leaders were clear regarding contact with such heathens. They were told that "even the acceptance of alms from a Samaritan delayed the redemption of Israel."[12]

Certainly no Jew would trouble himself to save a Samaritan life. The Samaritans had long ago split from the Israelites after being driven into exile following a war with the Babylonians. They had developed their own unique forms of worshipping Yhwh, which were seen as abhorrent by the Israelites. The fact that the third traveler was a Samaritan does not mean he was irreligious, but that his religion was *different*.

The word "Samaritan" is equated with "service and kindness" today, so perhaps for us to truly hear the message, we need to substitute for "Samaritan" a more modern example of someone we consider an enemy; someone like an "Al Qaeda loyalist" would perhaps help us feel the shock felt by the parable's earliest audience. Perhaps our trusted categories of people would begin to fall apart as well, if we read this parable helper as being this sort of enemy.

Maybe the Samaritan (or terrorist) stopped to help because he remembered times that he had felt the same vulnerability, fear, rejection, or violence as the man in the ditch. How honestly we are able to see ourselves will determine how clearly we will be able to see ourselves in the ditch. If what I claim about myself is shared with only a chosen few; if I limit my identity to external conditions such as race, gender, age, education, political party, nationality, income or religion, then my compassion, my ability to stand alongside anyone a bit different than myself, will be limited.

When we can imagine an enemy, usually someone as unlike ourselves as we imagine anyone could be, coming with compassion to our aide, then our compassion may, in turn, become limitless. Otherwise, we may find ourselves with those who ask, "Lord, when did we see you hungry and not give you food or thirsty and not give you something to drink?" (Matt 25:44)

The Book of Ruth in the Elder Testament is often seen as a bit of an odd story to find in the Bible since it does not even mention God. God doesn't do or say anything in the entire book of Ruth. But, if you look at the story of the "Good Samaritan" and the story of Ruth you will find some

---

12. Talbert, *Reading Luke*, 123.

Worldly Wisdom and Foolish Grace

remarkable similarities. Ruth, like the "Good Samaritan," belonged to a tribe of people that were the enemies of the Israelites.

Moses had declared, "You shall not abhor an Edomite, for he is your kinsman. You shall not abhor an Egyptian, for you were a stranger in his land. Children born to them may be admitted into the congregation of the Lord."(Deut 23:8–9).

Regarding a Moabite like Ruth, however, Moses said, "None of their descendants, even in the tenth generation, shall ever be admitted into the congregation of the Lord, because they did not meet you with food and water on your journey after you left Egypt, and because they hired Balaam . . . to curse you."(Deut 23:4–5).[13]

The story of Ruth begins with a man named Elimelech, an Israelite, of Bethlehem in Judah, who went to live in the enemy territory of Moab. Why did Elimalech choose Moab? Because, just like Abraham and the sons of Jacob had experienced, there was a famine in his land, so he went where there was food.

The commentaries of the rabbis come down pretty hard on Ebimelech, claiming that he was a deserter who turned his back on his own people just because he could afford the journey. They say that his name even suggests "self-aggrandizement," literally, "to me shall kingship come."

This story starts out badly and continues to get worse. The deserter Elimelech dies and his sons marry idol-worshipping Moabite women, instead of returning to their own monotheistic people, and then their Moabite wives remain childless, another disgrace in the eyes of his people.

When the sons of Ebimelech also die, the audience must have thought, "Now they will get out of this Moabite mess." Naomi, the widow of Ebimelech, decides to go back to Bethlehem. Not only is there food there now but, by returning, she can perhaps put right the disgrace of her husband's desertion. But as she prepares to head home, now knowing first-hand what it is like to live in exile, Naomi has compassion for her daughters-in-law, Orpah and Ruth, and tells them to let her make the journey home alone and to stay in their own land.

Orpah is "the majority of humankind living out its usualness on home ground."[14] Orpah decides to stay in Moab. None-the-less, she weeps and kisses Naomi goodbye. And then we come to Ruth.

---

13. Ozick, *Congregation*, 365.
14. Ozick, *Congregation*, 372.

Be a Good Neighbor

Cynthia Ozick reflects on what Ruth could have said to Naomi in "Congregation: Contemporary Writers Read the Jewish Bible." She could have been pragmatic and said "I am used to living in your household . . . It was you who completed my upbringing . . . so let me go with you." She could have been altruistic and said, "You are older in years than I . . . surely I will have a second chance, just as you predict, but you now, helpless as you are, how unprotected you will be! . . . Let me go and watch over you."

Instead, "the cosmic sweep of a single phrase transforms these spare syllables from the touching language of family feeling to the unearthly tongue of the visionary:"[15]

> Do not urge me to leave you, to turn back and not follow you. For wherever you go, I will go; wherever you lodge, I will lodge; your people shall be my people and your God my God. (Ruth 1:16)

Once again, it is an enemy of the Judean people, Ruth, like the Samaritan, who embodies the compassion of the one true God.

> Ruth's story is kindled into the Book of Ruth by the presence of God on Ruth's lips, (Ruth the Moabite enemy!) and her act is far, far more than a ringing embrace of Naomi, and far, far more than the simple acculturation it resembles. Ruth leaves Moab because she intends to leave childish ideas behind. She is drawn to Israel because Israel is the inheritor of the One Universal Creator.[16]

> It is said of the Prophet Muhammad, that as a funeral procession passed in front of him one day, he stood up. When someone told him that it was just the bier of a Jew he turned and asked that person, "Is it not a soul?"[17]

While humanity clings to what separates us as human beings, i.e., gender, age, religion, race, and other differences between us, the prophets of God teach that we are all alike; we are all children of One Creator. Until we can see ourselves in every other human being and in every human condition, we will not succeed in finding true compassion within.

> The story of the night journey reveals Muhammad's longing to bring the Arabs of the Hajiz, (partisan) who had felt that they had been left out of the divine plan, into the heart of the monotheistic family. This is a story of pluralism. Muhammad was abandoning

---

15. Ozick, *Congregation*, 377.
16. Ozick, *Congregation*, 377.
17 Cleary, *Wisdom*, 5.

the pagan pluralism of Mecca, because it had degenerated into the self-destructive arrogance and violence of jahiliyyah (the time and state of affairs before Islam), but he was beginning to embrace monotheistic pluralism. In Jerusalem, he discovered that all the prophets, sent by God to all peoples, are "brothers."[18]

Many of us remember how, as children, we fondly watched the TV Show "Mr. Rogers' Neighborhood." The host of this show, Mr. Fred Rogers, (1928–2003) who was a Presbyterian minister, dedicated his life to helping children understand that they need not fear people just because they seem different.

The story of Fred's life has been documented in two movies: "Won't You Be My Neighbor" in 2018 and "Beautiful Day in the Neighborhood" in 2019. Both titles are from his TV show theme song. Mr. Rogers sang this song as part of each episode that millions of children watched. It is a song that few of us will ever forget. Mr. Rogers encouraged every child in television-land to ask others to be their neighbor and to be a good neighbor themselves.

We are so fearful of people we do not know that we are quick to think, "Isn't inviting everyone to be your neighbor a dangerous thing to do? They could be bad people who could harm us." Today we tell children, "Don't talk to strangers." I'm not suggesting that we don't warn our children about dangerous situations, but only that looking at others as an opportunity to be a good neighbor, can be done safely.

Rabbi Jesus said that the greatest commandment is, "You shall love the LORD your God with all your heart, and with all your soul, and with all your mind, and with all your strength. The second is this, "You shall love your neighbor as yourself. There is no other commandment greater than these." (Mark 12:30–31) Mr. Rogers taught the same lesson by making the image of "neighbor" one that children would consider a good thing, a blessing, something to look for and create.

When I was five years old I looked forward to moving into a new house in a new neighborhood. I was a pretty adventurous child and took off down the sidewalk whenever I could escape my parents' watchful eyes. I escaped one day from my present house and headed off for my new house. I had gone about six blocks when, not far from my new home, I saw a young girl sitting on her front porch watching me. As I walked by she shouted, "Do you want to be my friend?" I shouted back, "Sure!" It

---

18. Armstrong, *Muhammad*, 85.

was the beginning of a dear friendship that lasts just as deeply today as ever, a true blessing in my life.

It is not enough to simply love those neighbors who we have gotten to know over years of living close to each other. We must begin to consider the people who we do not even know, who may live far away, and who, perhaps, we have never met, as neighbors also.

7

Turn the Other Cheek

It is good for a man, when young,
to bear a yoke;
let him sit alone and be patient,
when he has laid it upon him.
Let him put his mouth to the dust
there may yet be hope.
Let him offer his cheek to the smiter;
let him be surfeited with mockery.
For he does not reject forever,
but first afflicts, then pardons
in his abundant kindness,
for he does not willfully bring grief
or affliction to man, . . .

LAMENTATIONS 3:27–33[1]

You have heard that it was said, "An eye for an eye and a tooth for a tooth." But I say to you, Do not resist an evildoer. But if anyone strikes you on the right cheek, turn the other also; and if anyone wants to sue you and take your coat, give your cloak as well; and if anyone forces you to go one mile, go also the second mile.

---

1. Pelican, *Sacred*, 1434.

Give to everyone who makes a request of you, and do not turn away from or deny anyone who wants to borrow from you.

Matt 5: 38–42

The good deed and the evil deed are not equal.
Repel by that which is better;
then behold, the one between whom and thee there is enmity
shall be as if he were a loyal, protecting friend.
Yet none shall receive it, save those who are patient;
and none shall receive it, save those who possess great fortune.

Quran 41:34–35[2]

WORLDLY WISDOM—"AN EYE FOR AN EYE"

Gun Control and Capital Punishment.

Most cultures develop rules or standards that govern the interactions of their people. Some concept of an adequate payment or punishment for behavior that is hurtful or destructive has existed in most human civilizations. The simple idea of "an eye for an eye" has been helpful in many cultures for a long time as it helped determine what retribution or retaliation was reasonable. Many cultures still carry the almost instinctual belief that, if you hit me, it is natural and acceptable for me to hit you back.

Some communities and people attempt to live by different standards, such as "two wrongs don't make a right" and the Golden Rule of "Do unto others as you would have them do unto you" especially when trying to raise children who will behave peacefully. But we are still influenced by a "John Wayne meets Al Pacino meets Bruce Willis" message of "taking care" of those who threaten or harm us, or those we love, by retaliating with a vengeance.

Hollywood encourages the idea that vengeance is the right of the offended or of the friends of the victim by producing increasingly violent heroes who revel in bringing down the bad guys. Writers, producers, and directors seem to turn a blind eye to violence when it comes to making movies. The anger of violent "good guys" may feed our own hunger for

---

2. Nasr, *Quran*, 1165.

retaliation against those people, institutions, or communities that we feel have been unfair, unkind, or violent towards us.

The idea of "an eye for an eye" may have developed as early civilizations grew and less well-established systems for retribution led to on-going feuds which threatened the moral fabric of their society. Despite having been replaced with newer modes of legal theory, "eye for an eye" systems served a critical purpose in the establishment of a body whose purpose was to enact the penalty and ensure that theirs was the only penalty enforced. These bodies led to the development of "states."

The "eye for an eye" principle is found to have been part of the law in ancient Babylonia. The Babylonians came to understand that in societies which were not bound by the rule of law, if a person was hurt, the injured person or their relative could take retribution on the person who caused the injury. Such retribution was often worse than the initial crime, perhaps going as far as causing the death of the perpetrator.

The Younger Testament of Christian Scripture gives mixed messages about taking vengeance against those who wrong you. In his letter to the followers of "The Way" in Rome, the Apostle Paul wrote, "Beloved, never avenge yourselves, but leave room for the wrath of God; for it is written, 'Vengeance is mine, I will repay, says the LORD.'" (Rom 12:19) We were told not to exact retribution and that the LORD was the one who would "repay." But those who believed that they were created in the image of God must also have thought that, even though God would retaliate against those who did wrong, they also could be "God-like" and retaliate.

Gun violence continues to grow in our communities. It seems like news reports on mass shootings come faster and faster. Even as more people, including children and youth, speak out demanding legislators to, at the very least, limit and control the sales of automatic weapons, little has changed in our gun control laws.

It is not surprising that some of the people in our culture of vengeance are fighting for the right of every individual to bear arms. They end up wondering, after all, how they are going to defend themselves and their rights if they do not have the same weapons as those they fear.

Our nation is deeply divided over the issue of gun control. The National Rifle Association continues to expound on Second Amendment rights while an increasing number of innocent lives are lost.

Those who are in favor of gun control claim that more gun control would mean less guns getting into the hands of innocent children, who shoot themselves or others accidentally, or into the hands of those who are mentally ill, or agents of hate crimes, and end up killing others. Gun control advocates do not want to take away all guns, especially those used for hunting or protection, but specific types of automatic military weapons.

Those who are against gun control feel as if any limiting anyone's right to purchase any type of gun goes against the US Constitution. They claim that it is not the gun that kills but the one who shoots the gun.

The efficiency of the US Criminal Justice System has been the subject of debate for many years and the idea of "an eye for an eye" is often part of this discussion. On the other hand, when prisons or detention centers overflow with inmates, some judges are hesitant to give any prison sentences and some legislators are tempted to seek lesser mandatory sentencing laws.

Capital Punishment (Death Penalty) has been a part of that debate for centuries. Not only is this debate affected by ethical and religious beliefs, but by the attitude of the current culture due to experiences of death and dying caused by recent war or disease. For instance, the Constitutional Rights Foundation writes that, "The movement against the death penalty grew stronger after World War II, especially in Europe, where many were weary of so much killing during the war."[3]

The history of support for capital punishment has moved back and forth, for and against, over the years:

> In the American colonies, legal executions took place as early as 1630. As in England, the death penalty was imposed for many crimes, even minor ones such as picking pockets or stealing a loaf of bread. During the 1800s in England, for example, 270 crimes were capital offenses or crimes punishable by death. Thousands of people sometimes attended public hangings. Gradually, however, England and America reduced the number of capital offenses, until the main focus was on first-degree murder—murders showing deliberation, willfulness, and premeditation. They also moved executions within the walls of prisons to eliminate the spectacle of public executions.
>
> The 1950s and 1960s saw public protests over capital punishment and the number of executions in America gradually declined. In 1967 there were only two, and the following year saw the beginning of an unofficial moratorium on executions. States waited to see how the Supreme Court would rule on the constitutionality of

---

3. Constitutional, "History."

capital punishment. No executions took place in the United States from 1968 through 1976.

In the 1972 case of Furman v. Georgia, the Supreme Court declared capital punishment unconstitutional as it was then applied. The court said the death penalty was a violation of the Eighth Amendment prohibition against cruel and unusual punishment because of the inconsistency in who was given a death sentence and who was not. [4]

Since 1977 the death penalty has been upheld, reinstated or banned time and again by the US Supreme Court and various state legislators:

> Given the fallibility of human judgment, there has always been the danger that an execution could result in the killing of an innocent person. Nevertheless, when the U.S. Supreme Court held the administration of the death penalty to be unconstitutional in 1972, there was barely any mention of the issue of innocence in the nine opinions issued. Although mistakes were surely made in the past, the assumption prevailed that such cases were few and far between. Almost everyone on death row was "surely" guilty.
>
> However, as federal courts began to more thoroughly review whether state criminal defendants were afforded their guaranteed rights to due process, errors and official misconduct began to regularly appear, requiring retrials. When defendants were now afforded more experienced counsel, with fairly selected juries, and were granted access to scientific testing, some were acquitted and released. Since 1973, 166 former death-row prisoners have been exonerated of all charges and set free.[5]

Capital punishment is the most extreme form of retribution by a society for wrong doing. Even when enforced in only the most extreme cases of premeditated murder, capital punishment stands against the Ten Commandments passed down to Moses in which God declared that "You will not kill."(Exo 20:13)

The command not to kill and the necessity to go to war has led some interpreters to question if the commandment might really have meant, "You shall not murder." The argument, in this case, is that if we understand "murder" to mean "illegally" taking the life of another person and understand that killing on the battlefield is a "legal" act, then the commandment not to kill does not apply to warfare.

4. Constitutional, "History."
5. Death Penalty, "Innocence."

FOOLISH GRACE—"TURN THE OTHER CHEEK"

Matthew 5:38–42

> You have heard that it was said, "An eye for an eye and a tooth for a tooth." But I say to you, do not resist an evildoer. But if anyone strikes you on the right cheek, turn the other also; and if anyone wants to sue you and take your coat, give your cloak as well; and if anyone forces you to go one mile, go also the second mile. Give to everyone who makes a request of you, and do not turn away from or deny anyone who wants to borrow from you.

The Jesus Seminar scholars gave their first place award for most authentic text from Rabbi Jesus to most of this text from Matthew.[6] The phrase, "You have heard it said" is used by Matthew to link together a series of Rabbi Jesus' teachings. The phrase could have been the author's creative device or how Jesus himself introduced these lessons, but in either case, the phrase, "You have heard it said" always refers to a common cultural understanding and not to words of Torah. The biblical phrase, "It is written" is used when referring to Torah.[7]

Jesus understood that Torah, the rule he lived by, had no room for the concept of "an eye for an eye." The concept that enacting any sort of retribution would repay or restore the victim is foreign to Torah's understanding of reciprocal justice. In Torah, victims are instructed not even to hate or hold anything against those who have harmed them.

In this lesson, Rabbi Jesus corrects the common misunderstanding and cultural twisting of one of Moses' teachings. In the book of Exodus, the story is told of Moses instructing the community of former Hebrew slaves to follow a legal system of penalties and reparations. He declares that a fine should be paid for a lost pregnancy that is the result of a fight between others. The fine may be set by the pregnant woman's husband but must be agreed upon by the judges. A further penalty could also be set for any further harm that comes to the woman, appropriate in measure to the harm inflicted. (Exo 21:22–25)

Directly following this text, Moses gave two more examples of how the metaphor "an eye for an eye and a tooth for a tooth" was to be applied when

---

6. Funk, *Five Gospels*, 143.
7. Funk, *Five Gospels*, 145.

bodily harm to a servant was involved. While still in the wilderness these ex-slaves clearly had quickly established a hierarchy of servitude:

> When a slave owner strikes the eye of a male or female slave, destroying it, the owner shall let the slave go, a free person, to compensate for the eye. If the owner knocks a tooth out of a male or female slave, the slave shall be let go, a free person, to compensate for the tooth.
> (Exo 21:26–27)

"An eye for an eye" was not meant to be taken literally. The slave owner was not asked to take out his own eye if he destroyed his slave's eye but to let the slave go free in compensation for the damage done to the eye.

Letting a slave go free may not seem like a harsh enough penalty for the slave owner to bear when compared to destroying the slave's eye, but it did cost the slave owner the value of the slave's work for a lifetime. In the case of knocking out a slave's tooth, some slave owners may have preferred to follow the regulation literally and take out one of their own teeth rather than set their slave free. In other words, some punishments may actually have been harsher than the literal "eye for an eye" payment.

Can you imagine the slave owners of our nation's early history agreeing to let a slave go free because they had caused that slave some form of harm? These Christian people used scripture to claim that God allowed the practice of owning slaves, but not the text in Exodus where Moses prescribed the laws of retribution toward slaves.

The idea of not applying any retribution at all, but "turning the other cheek" was such a radical idea to propose to the ancient Middle Eastern audience of Rabbi Jesus, that many biblical scholars have decided that these challenging instructions should be understood as politically strategic rather than purely compassionate. It is hard for any of us to imagine that Rabbi Jesus would ask those who were being persecuted to take even more abuse from their persecutors:

> The Sermon on the Mount is Rabbi Jesus at his ornery best; offering "advice" that makes no sense divorced from the nature of the one giving it. Such confusing and passive directions that challenged the people to do the exact opposite of what seemed normal and reasonable, must be understood contextually, and must have something to do with political strategy; must have been meant to catch their enemies off guard, to weaken the position of their persecutors.[8]

---

8. Byassee, "Seventh Sunday," 382.

Turn the Other Cheek

There is an interesting contextual argument of those who consider this lesson to be purely strategic. For those in the ancient Middle East, slapping someone's cheek with the back of your hand was very demeaning. Picture it. It was always the right cheek of the one who was slapped and the back of the slapper's right hand that did the slapping. If you turned the "left" cheek to be slapped, the slapper would find it difficult to slap with the back of their right hand. (You may need to try this out, gently, with a partner.) "Turning the other cheek," in other words, may not have been submissive, some contend, but actually might have caused the slapper some embarrassment as he contorted his arm and body to throw the second blow.

Their arguments include the idea that most people owned only two garments in that culture. To strip naked would "uncover," so to speak, the judiciary injustice of the one making the request. Also, Roman soldiers were allowed by law to enlist a local citizen to carry their gear for one mile only; going a second might put the soldier in trouble with the law.[9]

Professor Greg Carey also believes that this lesson is strategic:

> It is as if (Rabbi Jesus) were saying, "When you cannot force people to treat you justly, you can expose the injustice of the situation. When striking back will only get you hurt, confront the aggressor without retaliating. When your debts are out of control, show how your poverty leaves you without protection from the elements. When your occupier demands your labor, put him in an impossible situation by going beyond conventional expectations."[10]

Professor Walter Wink agrees, calling Jesus' way, "The Third Way." "To an oppressed people, Jesus is saying, "Do not continue to acquiesce in your oppression by the Powers; but do not react violently to it either. Rather, find a third way, a way that is neither submission nor assault, flight nor fight, a way that can secure your human dignity and begin to change the power equation, even now, before the revolution."[11]

This teaching from Rabbi Jesus should be commended not just because it seems so authentic but due to the depth of powerful lessons it teaches.

The lessons we could take from this text include:

1. Do not abuse Torah by interpreting lines of text to your own advantage.
2. Extend compassion and go beyond what is expected.

---

9. Levine, *Jewish Annotated*, 12.
10. Carey, "Seventh Sunday," 381, 383.
11. Wink, *Powers*, 110.

3. Use non-violent ways to acquire justice and reconciliation.
4. Do not to return evil for evil, but return evil with good.

None of the gospel writers actually record Rabbi Jesus as saying, "Do not return evil for evil," yet, in other writings from the first century there is strong evidence that Rabbi Jesus taught non-violence like other Judean teachers. In the Dead Sea Scrolls, a parchment was discovered called the "Rules of the Community" which are thought to include many ideas that Rabbi Jesus taught. The tenth rule reads: "I will pay to no man the reward of evil; I will pursue him with goodness. For judgment of all the living is with God and it is (God) who will render to man (sic) his reward."[12]

The Apostle Paul wrote about retribution in a letter to followers of The Way in Rome:

> Do not repay anyone one evil for evil, but take thought to what is noble in the sight of all. If it is possible, so far as it depends on you, live peaceably with all. Beloved, never avenge yourselves, but leave room for the wrath of God; for it is written, "Vengeance is mine, I will repay, says the LORD." No, if your enemy is hungry, feed them; if they are thirsty, give them something to drink; for by doing this you will heap burning coals on their heads. Do not be overcome by evil, but overcome evil with good. (Rom 12:17–21)

The phrase "an eye for an eye and the whole world goes blind" was coined by Mahatma Gandhi in reference to his campaign for non-violence in solving oppression and persecution in India and winning India's independence from the United Kingdom. Gandhi encouraged people to see that violent retribution only perpetuated itself and never led to resolution of violence and suffering.

"An eye for eye and a tooth for tooth" has been quoted often as justification for vengeance rather than as an understanding of equitable justice. Instead of thinking in literal terms of the minimum one should be repaid if harmed, or of the limits of the penalty they should pay for harm inflicted, Rabbi Jesus challenged his followers to think about justice, about what is the equitable, fair, and compassionate behavior they should exhibit. Instead of: "I should get to slap someone who slaps me," or "If someone takes my coat, I should be allowed to take their coat," Rabbi Jesus asks us to think: "How can I be compassionate in this situation?" The idea that "turning the other cheek" may have been somewhat strategic in causing the enemy some

---

12. Vermes, "Rules," Col X, #18.

sort of discomfort or legal issue may not be completely off the mark, but only in terms of getting the enemy to rethink their behavior in order to de-escalate the situation.

There are many differences between what we think of as "fair" or "just" and what we would consider compassionate. Capital punishment is still considered "just" and "ethical" by many and compassionate for the victims, but is it compassionate toward the perpetrators? If a person who is house-less sleeps in a restricted area in a park or on a public sidewalk, it may be legal to force them to move because they are breaking the law, but is it compassionate?

Rabbi Jesus asked the people to go beyond the required expectations of their culture, to go beyond what most other people might have done in a given situation, and to live, instead, with a heart of generosity, tolerance, and understanding.

Rabbi Jesus understood the power of oppressed people through the image of the suffering servant the Prophet Isaiah, "I did not hide my face from insult and spitting . . . I have set my face like flint, and I know that I shall not be put to shame."(Isa 50:6–7) In similar words in the book of Lamentations, we read, "Let him give his cheek to the one who strikes him, and be filled with insults." (Lam 3:30)

The biblical Book of Lamentations was written after Jerusalem was destroyed and the Holy Temple burned to the ground by the Babylonians in 586 BCE. Lamentations tells of Jerusalem's misery and the Lord's anger, of Judah's complaint against the Lord as well as their seeking the Lord's forgiveness. These are the feelings, words, and images of an ancient people who had no other explanation in which to live and face an unknown future than God's righteousness, God's anger at injustice, and God's promised grace and forgiveness.

Many people of faith no longer believe that the Creator God causes bad things to happen to people but only that bad things happen, sometimes due to our action or inaction and sometimes regardless of what we do. Even so, we can easily imagine the feelings of the people who were living in Jerusalem when the Babylonians invaded. Those who survived the invasion hid and watched as their city and temple were leveled and as their neighbors and family members were marched off in bondage to serve as slaves of their enemies in lands far away.

Though the author is anonymous, some think it was the Prophet Jeremiah who speaks in Lamentations:

Worldly Wisdom and Foolish Grace

> How lonely sits the city that once was full of people! How like a widow she has become, she that was great among the nations! She that was a princess among the provinces has become a vassal. (Lam 1:1) What can I say for you, to what compare you, O daughter Jerusalem? To what can I liken you, that I may comfort you, O virgin daughter Zion? For vast as the sea is your ruin; who can heal you? (Lam 2:13)

Even in their despair; even as they could not envision any hope, eventually the broken and suffering people began to remember the story of God's redemption of their ancestors from Egypt. They recalled the stories of God rebuilding and restoring their nation again and again, and they began to repeat words of remembrance and hope to each other. The lamenting ended and a new day began:

> The thought of my affliction and my homelessness is wormwood and gall! My soul continually thinks of it and is bowed down within me. But this I call to mind, and therefore I have hope: The steadfast love of the LORD never ceases, his mercies never come to an end; they are new every morning; great is your faithfulness. "The LORD is my portion," says my soul, "therefore I will hope in him." (Lam 3:19–24)

Suddenly they began to see beyond their suffering: "It is good for one to bear the yoke in youth, to sit alone in silence when the LORD has imposed it." (Lam 3:27–28) They decided to persist in calling on God for they knew God's help would eventually come.

As part of this dealing with struggle while holding onto hope, other images also came to mind: "to put one's mouth to the dust, to give one's cheek to the smiter, and be filled with insults, for the LORD will not reject forever." (Lam 3:29–31) Could these have been the images used by the prophet that Jesus remembered when he instructed his disciples to turn the other check?

In *Surah* (or chapter) 41, verses 34 and 35 of the Quran, the Prophet Muhammad reveals the words of Allah regarding how to respond to evil:

> The good deed and the evil deed are not equal.
> Repel by that which is better;
> then behold, the one between whom and thee there is enmity
> shall be as if he were a loyal, protecting friend.
> Yet none shall receive it, save those who are patient;
> and none shall receive it, save those who possess great fortune.
> Quran 41:34–35[13]

---

13. Nasr, *Quran*, 1165.

Turn the Other Cheek

Was this Allah's response to another culture who believed in "an eye for an eye"? This text from the Quran seems to be saying that an evil deed does not become a good deed simply because it is considered equal retaliation. This is another way of saying, "Violence is evil regardless of the reason behind the violence"?

Allah says, "Repel by that which is better." It seems awkward to non-Arabic ears to read a phrase which doesn't include a direct object that is to be repelled. To western ears this leaves it up to the reader to decide what might be repelled. Perhaps anger should be repelled by patience or error by truth . . . *Better* can also mean "more beautiful or more virtuous:"

> To repel evil with good does not mean to surrender before one's enemy or to accept falsehood over truth, but instead to avoid reciprocating harm whenever such avoidance will not lead to greater evil. In this vein, a *hadith* taken by many as a foundational principle of Islam states, "Let there be no harming and no reciprocating harm."[14]

The Quran continues with "then, behold, the one between whom and thee there is enmity shall be as if he were a loyal, protecting friend." Even though some claim that Rabbi Jesus said to turn the other check as a strategic act to embarrass or disgrace an opponent, it is clear here that the ultimate reason for a non-violent response was to turn an opponent into a friend.

Verse 35 includes a final word of caution, "the small print" of a disclaimer: "Yet none shall receive it, save those that are patient; and none shall receive it, save those who possess great fortune." The "it" in this disclaimer is not specific but probably refers to the loyalty and protection of the new friend that results from "repelling by that which is better." "Great fortune" means much more than "good luck." It means that such an end to enmity can only be achieved by those who have "an abundance of intellect and vision, or a high degree of virtue, spiritual strength, and inner purity . . . or who possess Paradise."[15]

The prophets of the Elder Testament may have taught Rabbi Jesus and the Prophet Muhammad alike, to live their lives and give their lives embracing the divine power of not returning evil with evil, of returning good in the face of evil, or, in other words, of loving enemies and loving beyond cultural expectations.

---

14. Nasr, *Quran*, 1165.
15. Nasr, *Quran*, 1165.

Worldly Wisdom and Foolish Grace

"Foolish grace" asks that we let go of self-protection and self-interest, in order to respond to others purely with the goal of ending the violence, the enmity, the conflict, and creating peace and understanding in its place. "Foolish grace" leads us to sacrifice the self for the good of the other and the community as a whole.

8

Love and Bless Your Enemies

If you see the donkey of one who hates you
lying down under its burden,
you shall refrain from leaving him with it;
you shall rescue it with him.

EXODUS 23:4–5[1]

You have heard that it was said, "You shall love your neighbor and hate your enemy." But I say to you, Love your enemies and pray for those who persecute you, so that you may be children of your Father in heaven; for he makes his sun rise on the evil and on the good, and sends rain on the righteous and on the unrighteous. For if you love those who love you, what reward do you have? Do not even the tax-collectors do the same?"

MATTHEW 5:43–46

And hold fast to the rope of God, all together, and be not divided;
Remember the blessing of God upon you, when you were enemies
and He joined your hearts, such that you became brothers by His blessing.
You were on the brink of a pit of fire and He delivered you from it.

---

1. Pelican, *Sacred*, 120.

Thus does God make clear unto you His signs,
that haply you may be rightly guided.

QURAN 3:103[2]

WORLDLY WISDOM—"FEAR, HATRED, AND RETALIATION"

Travel Bans, Crusades, and Racism

As the US declared its independence from England in 1776, the leaders of a new nation affirmed certain truths, the most important of which was, that all persons are created equal and are endowed by God with certain inalienable rights. We have been arguing about the limits of and exceptions to those rights, and who is considered part of the "all people" of this declaration, ever since.

From the day foreign explorers first stepped onto North America, "all" neglected to include the indigenous, First Nations people, as well as women, children, slaves, immigrants from Europe and the other Americas, people with physical and mental challenges, religious minorities, the poor, and the under-educated.

The "all" in our founders' statement on equality seems to have meant little more than "all of those like us," i.e., "white men." We continue to argue about which of "us" are to be trusted—and therefore welcomed and protected—and which of "them" are dangerous—and therefore must be kept at a distance.

Our best intentions to insure justice and equality are silenced by our fears. Our instinct is to protect ourselves, our families, and communities from any perceived harm on the part of strange, and therefore suspicious, people. Rather than taking the time to clearly discern if there is any real danger inherent in a strange person, "others" are considered dangerous and not entitled to the equality that we value for ourselves.

Perhaps a most blatant example of our fear of the other—the "not like us,"—is the proclamation made by the POTUS in December of 2015 that called for a complete ban on travel to the United States on the part of anyone from countries that he considered mostly Muslim.

---

2. Nasr, *Quran*, 158–59.

Love and Bless Your Enemies

The reason for Trump's ban was that because *some* people who followed the religion of Islam had committed violent acts against the US, *all* Muslims were to be feared and therefore denied entrance into the US. Similar examples of cultural fear of the stranger can be found throughout human history.

When Rabbi Jesus came to the synagogue and unrolled the scroll to read from the Prophet Isaiah, the people asked, "Is this not Joseph's son?" Rabbi Jesus said to them, "Doubtless you will say, 'Doctor, cure yourself! Do here the things we heard that you did in Capernaum.'" Hearing this, Jesus reminded the people that the prophet Elijah had healed the son of the widow of Zarephath, in the land of Sidon (I Kgs 17:8–24) and Elisha, had healed the military leader Naaman, an Aramean. (2 Kgs 5:1–19)

The people of Nazareth who heard this from Rabbi Jesus were offended. They assumed that the healing of the God of Israel would go, initially and foremost, to the people of Israel. That some of God's prophets would even speak of such healing for outsiders rather than their own people, was blasphemy! Some of the people of Nazareth became so angry at the thought of such blasphemy that they tried to hurl Rabbi Jesus off a cliff. (Luke 4:1–30)

At the start of the eleventh century, Muslim Turks from central Asia moved west and began to settle in lands that were inhabited by Greek Christians. A hundred years later, Pope Urban organized the first crusade to drive the Muslim settlers out of those provinces east of Rome which had come to belong to the Roman Empire.

Pope Urban and the Christian Roman Empire needed access to the holy Christian sites which were in Jerusalem and had come under Muslim control. The Church continued its murderous crusades against Islam for eight centuries.

Out of fear, racism has continued to legitimize injustice, oppression, and genocide. The nationalism of white supremacy in Germany and Poland in the 1930s "legally" massacred millions of people considered undesirable including Jews, others of non-Aryan races, and sexual minorities. Many "good, upright, law abiding citizens" of the US have violently resisted civil rights legislation ever since Africans were first kidnapped and brought to the US to work and live as slaves.

As long as men control most of the business, education, medicine, and governmental agencies in the US, women will continue to be treated as second-class citizens. As women slowly became part of the workforce, like their male counterparts, they gained rights previously held only by men, such as the right to own property and the right to vote. As long as heterosexual people are self-serving and remain in positions of power, homosexual citizens will continue to be considered, by many, as less-worthy to receive the same rights as the majority. Politically, fear of the "other" in the 1950s created hearings led by Senator McCarthy and others which targeted, oppressed, and imprisoned anyone suspected of even befriending a communist, let alone anyone who professed to hold such ideas.

Why are we so afraid of anyone who is "different?" Researchers have discovered some interesting facts about how human nature deals with the concept of "them" and "us." For instance, it is shockingly quick and easy to establish "them" and "us." Experiments which assigned half a group of people to a Blue Team and half to a Red Team discovered that as soon as the team groupings were set people started showing a preference toward people on their team. They immediately liked their team members better and spent more time interacting with each other than with the other team. However, if they stopped the game, said a mistake had been made in the team assignments, and moved a person from one team to the other, the reassigned person would suddenly begin to act as if they liked their new team better.

In other experiments, researchers found that participants rated the other team as having fewer good qualities. In the end, our brain tells us to fear those who are not perceived "as good as" our team. As we begin to fear the other, we tend to exaggerate the threats they may bring to us. Our brains work hard at protecting "us" from "them."

Since people tend to pay more attention to brief sound bites or anecdotes than to longer explanations, those with agendas set on spreading fear, persuade through headlines that are false but "catchy": "Immigrants from Mexico are taking jobs away from Americans!" "Islam commands its followers to kill non-believers!" "Homosexuals are child-molesters!"

With so much working against the use of rational thought and data, it is amazing that researchers have also found that it is fairly easy to end fear of the stranger. One powerful tool that can change one's perception is as simple as looking at a personal picture or hearing a personal story about the other's life; in other words, "putting a human face on it."

The news photo of the lifeless body of a dead child lying on a US beach is forever imprinted on many of our minds. The article with the picture reported that the child's family had joined a crowded boat of people fleeing their country for safety in the US and that the boat had capsized. An innocent child, along with others, had drowned. Even though this led many people to feel great compassion for the child, such pictures did not change the thoughts of many conservative legislators when considering immigration reform.

Putting a personal face on the "other" may change our perception, but only if we do it in person and spend time getting to know the person and their situation. Meeting and talking to a stranger can eliminate fears held for a lifetime. As we begin to see that they are a lot more like us than we ever imagined, we begin to understand that we are all, in fact, marked with the same divine image.

Webster's Dictionary defines *enemy* as "1: one that is antagonistic to another, *esp*: one seeking to injure, overthrow, or confound an opponent, 2: something harmful or deadly 3: a: a military adversary b: a hostile unit or force."[3] It seems logical that we would feel fear, contempt, and hatred of those who we call our enemies.

When someone seeks to harm us, we typically do not feel any comfort or safety with them. If someone chases after us on the playground every day, trying to push us into the dirt, we are probably not going to want to be around them. We might even begin to think about what we could do to hurt them in return, that seems only natural and understandable, right?

Such hatred of perceived enemies is a human trait that serves to protect people from getting hurt again and again by the same people. When I hate my enemy, I stay far away from them and I try to stop them from being able to hurt me or those I care about in the future.

Sometimes, on the other hand, we have to be "taught" to hate and fear the "other" and most especially those others considered enemies. If a child, for instance, has never experienced any aggression or harm from a stranger, they are likely to walk up to them boldly, with no fear at all. But when our parents quickly come to take us away from those people and start telling us about "stranger danger" we begin to think twice about who we can trust and the "us" becomes a much smaller circle of people.

Teaching "stranger danger" is a sad necessity in our communities today and needs to be explained carefully to children. As children grow the subtle complexities of such "rules" can be explained so that children can see that differences do not *always* mean we need to be wary.

---

3. Merriam, *Webster's Ninth*, 412.

Worldly Wisdom and Foolish Grace

Most US citizens felt as if they knew who the enemy was when they witnessed the attack on the twin towers of the World Trade Center in New York City and the Pentagon in Maryland on September 11, 2001. Those who piloted the three suicide planes that exploded into those buildings, killing thousands, became our enemies in an instant. But who were they exactly? Angry Muslims filled with hatred against the US? Syrians? Iraqis? Afghans? American Muslims fighting for some Middle Eastern madman?

As I remember, it didn't matter much that we who witnessed the horror didn't know exactly who they were. All we knew at first was that we suddenly had some real, visible enemies. What most people wanted to know was how "we" were going to protect ourselves from future attacks. Many people just wanted to know how "we" were going to make "them" pay for the lives they had taken.

Very quickly some people started fearing that every mosque in the country could be a place where "enemies" plotted against "us." American-Muslim neighbors on our streets were suspected of planning another attack. Mosques were targeted for attack by American extremists. Some non-Muslim Americans could not consider that any of the people worshipping in Mosques had actually been born and raised in America. All those US citizens, or at least US residents, in Mosques had become "the enemy."

When the Japanese military bombed Pearl Harbor on December 7, 1941, the US sent many Japanese Americans to internment camps believing suddenly that "they" were our enemies. Those of Japanese ancestry who wanted to fight alongside their American neighbors in defense of the US, their country, were told they could not serve because "they" were now our enemy.

Some enemies are not so easy to recognize. For some people, anyone working in an abortion clinic is an enemy. But how do you recognize these people once they walk out the doors of the clinic? At least eleven people have been killed in attacks on abortion clinics in the US since 1993 because people felt that "those people" inside an abortion clinic were the enemy.

In many white communities, a person with dark skin is suspected of being less trustworthy than a person with lighter skin. In many middle and upper class neighborhoods anyone living on the streets is suspected of being someone a bit suspect, who might steal anything they can and destroy our property. Many Democrats today consider that our country's real enemies are the Republicans and vice versa.

Love and Bless Your Enemies

Conspiracy theorists say that doctors, lawyers, politicians, business owners, scientists, policemen, investigators, the food industry, pharmaceuticals, health clubs, and those in many other professions are not to be trusted; many feel that there are people and organizations "out to get us" and we must fight against them or we will fall prey to their evil intentions.

Far too many people are coming to believe that there is really no one left to trust in this world. Worldly wisdom is now: "Everyone for them self," "Arm yourselves for the battle," and "You can't trust anyone these days."

FOOLISH GRACE—"LOVE AND BLESS YOUR ENEMIES"
Matthew 5:43–46

> "You have heard that it was said, 'You shall love your neighbor and hate your enemy.' But I say to you, Love your enemies and pray for those who persecute you, so that you may be children of your Father in heaven; for he makes his sun rise on the evil and on the good, and sends rain on the righteous and on the unrighteous. For if you love those who love you, what reward do you have? Do not even the tax-collectors do the same?"

The scholars of the Jesus Seminar worked long and hard before they voted on the authenticity of biblical quotes from Rabbi Jesus. They printed the most authentic texts in bright red letters in their translation of the Gospels. Bright red means "Pay close attention. No pansy pink here!"

These scholars concluded that the phrase "Love your enemies" ranks third highest among biblical sayings that most likely originated with Rabbi Jesus.[4] "Love your enemies" is part of the list of teachings from Rabbi Jesus, each of which is framed with the words, "You have heard it said . . . , but I say to you . . ."

In this list of saying from Rabbi Jesus that Matthew compiled, Rabbi Jesus also teaches about anger being as destructive as murder and lust being as dangerous as adultery. Jesus questions the escape clauses given for divorce and for swearing oaths and finally advises nonresistance to evildoers. Professor Amy Jill Levine writes that to consider these saying "antitheses," or contradictions of Torah, as many Christian scholars have done, is inaccurate, for the sayings actually only intensify the teachings of Torah.[5]

---

4. Funk, *Five Gospels*, 149.
5. Levine, *Jewish Annotated*, 11.

The phrase, "You have heard it said . . ." does not refer to Torah. When referring to Torah, the words, "It is written . . ." are used as the introduction. The Jesus Seminar translated the NRSV phrase, as "As you know, we once were told, . . ." instead of "You have heard that it was said," to make this clearer to the readers.[6]

In this lesson, Rabbi Jesus was not referring to a law that the people had received from Torah but to a "human precept" developed over time through assumptions being made within their culture and community. Many people had confused teachings from Torah with traditions of the community, both of which were being taught by their elders.

Rabbi Jesus tried to both clarify and perfect the understanding of Torah. He believed that Torah clearly taught: "You shall love your neighbor." The Elder Testament Book of "Leviticus," states that: "You shall not take vengeance or bear a grudge against any of your people, but you shall love your neighbor as yourself: I am the LORD."(Lev 19:18)

The second part of Matt 5:43: "and hate your enemy," is found nowhere in Torah. Jewish commentator, Dr. J. H. Hertz, C.H., the late Chief Rabbi of the British Empire, called this statement by Matthew "partisan" and "invented to depreciate the Torah."[7] Unfortunately, Rabbi Hertz knew that Christian scholars of his day were claiming that "You have heard it said" meant that the second phrase, "hate your enemy," was also found in Torah. Christian scholars today realize that this is not the case.

Hertz went on to explain that the book of Exodus clearly teaches love of enemies. In Exodus, Moses declares the civil regulations that God had handed down on Mt. Sinai:

> When you come upon your enemy's ox or donkey going astray, you shall bring it back. When you see the donkey of one who hates you lying under its burden, and you would hold back from setting it free, you must help to set it free. (Exo 23:4–5)

Hertz explains this text writing that, "He has not ceased to be your fellow man because he violates the law of neighborly love towards you. Therefore, all envy or ill-will toward him is forbidden. No thought of vengeance must be permitted to rise in your heart."[8]

---

6. Funk, *Five Gospels*, 145.
7. Hertz, *Pentateuch*, 316.
8. Hertz, *Pentateuch*, 316.

Love and Bless Your Enemies

No text in the Younger Testament could have caused more potential conflict between Jews and Christians than this misguided interpretation of Matthew 5:43. Rabbi Hertz tells of the conflict it caused by quoting C.G. Montefiore, the intellectual founder of Anglo-Liberal Judaism, the fourth largest Jewish denomination in England from 1858 to1938:

> Montefiore claimed that "we cannot think very highly of the morality of that New Testament author in inventing a sentence unknown to the Torah in order to depreciate the Torah.... The adherents of no religion have hated their enemies more than Christians. The atrocities which they have committed in the name of religion, both inside and outside their own pale, are unexampled in the world's history."[9]

There is much debate over whether Matthew thought that the phrase "hate your enemies" was found in Torah, but it is clear that Antisemitism influenced many parts of the Gospel. Most Christian scholars today have made it clear that "You have heard that is was said," refers to cultural messages rather than Torah. Christians are called to do all they can to correct such misunderstandings of Scripture and to read scripture with ears attuned to possible polemics of the writers.

Many texts in the Elder Testament clearly teach love of enemies. Proverbs teaches, "Do not rejoice when your enemies fall, and do not let your heart be glad when they stumble, or else the Lord will see it and be displeased, and turn away his anger from them." (Prov 24:17) Rabbi Jesus reminded his students about the true teaching of Torah and perhaps even broadened the application of those lessons:

> But I say to you love your enemies and bless those who curse you and do what is pleasing to those who hate you and pray for those who take you by force and persecute you.
> (Matt 5:44)[10]

We find similar sayings from other teachers of Jesus' day, many of whom were working to correct human precepts that had developed regarding the Mosaic Law:

---

9. Hertz, *Pentateuch*, 316.
10. Younan, "Peshitta."

Worldly Wisdom and Foolish Grace

Jesus, Hillel, Gamliel, Shammai, Akiva, Yokhann ben Zakkai, Shimon bar Yochai, and Judah HaNasi were in the midst of one of the major paradigm shifts in Jewish history.[11]

The "sages" referred to in Jewish commentary and literature, were those authoritative and trusted teachers in ancient times who interpreted the words of Torah. Most of the final opinions of these sages is recorded in a collection of writings called the Talmud. One such writing is Baba Metzia 32b in which the sage considers the commands given to help others in need:

> "Come and hear: If a friend requires unloading, and an enemy loading, one's [first] obligation is towards his enemy, in order to subdue his evil inclinations."[12]

Perhaps this wise counsel was given to emphasize that helping those in need was such a priority in faithful, compassionate living, that the people were expected to help their enemies, even if it meant putting themselves in some possible harm, for it might also have the effect of making that enemy feel less hatred toward or hold less "evil inclinations" toward you. These sages advised that:

> "all other things being equal, if there is a choice between helping an enemy and helping a friend, helping an enemy takes precedence since it may 'overcome the inclination', that is, it may help end the animosity and turn an enemy into a friend."[13]

The people who sat at the feet of the Prophet Muhammad had lived with tribal enemies all their lives. Tribal and religious warfare was everywhere. No one felt safe outside of their own village or home, if they lived in the city:

> This was a frightening period. The incessant wars between Persia and Byzantium seemed to herald the end of the old world order, and even within Arabia, tribal warfare had reached chronic proportions. During the last twenty years, the Ghazu, (common attacks against other tribes) which had traditionally been short and sharp, had escalated into long, drawn out military campaigns as a result of unprecedented drought and famine. There was an apocalyptic sense of impending catastrophe. Muhammad was

---

11. Zaslow, *Jesus*, 37.
12. Baba Metzia, para 2 from end.
13. Sacks, "Socialism," para 5.

Love and Bless Your Enemies

convinced that unless the Quraysh reformed their attitudes and behavior, they too world fall prey to the anarchy that threated to engulf the world.[14]

The Prophet Muhammad was sent as a young child to be raised by a Bedouin tribe called the Quraysh, who attempted to live by nomadic customs. Nomadic life was a struggle between tribes, filled with endless raids during times of scarcity and starvation, to steal precious resources of water and pastureland. Most of these raids carefully avoided any killing which would instigate revenge and further killing and were an accepted practice that redistributed the resources among the tribes.

The Quraysh tribe eventually managed to save enough surplus resources permitting them to move closer to a city and a more settled way of life. They had slowly become independent traders who had little time or energy to cultivate land. They had to depend on trading for food and water. Instead of depending on their agricultural, nomadic customs, they had to cultivate a way of peaceful coexistence that made business ventures more stable. At the same time, as the Quraysh became wealthy on their trade routes and less vulnerable, they turned away from helping others around them:[15]

> . . . the Quraysh despised the weak; they believed that failure and poverty revealed an inherent lack of nobility, so they felt no obligation towards the poor, the orphan, or the widow. But if they understood their dependence upon Allah at every moment of their lives, they would appreciate their own frailty, and their arrogance would be tempered by awe and wonder. They would lay aside their haughty self-reliance and their proudly cultivated refusal to bow to any creature, human or divine. Muhammad wanted every man, woman, and child in Mecca to develop within themselves the humble thankfulness that should characterize the human condition.[16]

With the above words, Armstrong summarizes Muhammad's entire mission and message. This was the same mission and message of the prophets that came before him: "Humble thankfulness to the One God that leads to compassion for all other creatures."

In 610 CE, when Muhammad was making his annual pilgrimage to Mount Hira, it is said that he was dramatically "attacked" by an angel of

---

14. Armstrong, *Muhammad*, 44.
15. Armstrong, *Muhammad*, 18–19.
16. Armstrong, *Muhammad*, 52.

Worldly Wisdom and Foolish Grace

Allah and that "words were squeezed, as from the depths of his being." Muhammad was illiterate; he could neither read nor write, but he felt convicted to speak the words he heard that day:

> Recite in the name of your LORD who created—
> From an embryo created the human.
> Recite you LORD is all-giving
> Who taught by the pen
> Taught the human what he did not know before
> The human being is a tyrant
> He thinks his possessions make him secure
> To your LORD is the return of everything.[17]

This LORD "who taught by the pen, (who) taught the human what he did not know before" is the same LORD God who inspired the words of prophets and patriarchs, rabbis and redeemers, authors and editors, 600 years before Muhammad. During the six centuries following the death of Rabbi Jesus, the world had become a new place; many more people in Arabia were living comfortably with greater wealth. It seems clear that the message of the Abrahamic tradition had finally found just the right prophet for this new time and place in Muhammad!

Just as Moses had felt when he was sent to redeem the Hebrew slaves out of Egypt, the Prophet Muhammad felt totally inadequate when Allah sent him to witness to the Quraysh; he felt that there was no way that he could follow in the footsteps of Abraham, Moses, and Jesus. It took some time before he ventured out with God's message even to his closest relatives and friends.

When Mohammad finally shared his revelation from Mount Hira, most of his clan turned on him, also believing that he couldn't possibly be Allah's messenger. They considered his words presumptuous blasphemy. It took years of struggle, (in Arabic, *jihad*) before Mohammad slowly drew a group of followers who also saw the need to turn from centering only on their own lives.

Some who came to sit at the feet of Mohammad had most likely been enemies not long before, their tribes having fought, first for valuable resources, and eventually for power and wealth:

> And hold fast to the rope of God, all together, and be not divided;
> Remember the blessing of God upon you, when you were enemies
> and He joined your hearts, such that you became brothers by His blessing.

---

17 Armstrong, *Muhammad*, 33–34.

> You were on the brink of a pit of fire and He delivered you from it.
> Thus does God make clear unto you His signs,
> that haply you may be rightly guided.
> Quran 3:103[18]

Muhammad's message of selfless love made it possible for ancient enemies to become friends—a community devoted to following the One God. It would be Muhammad's mission and message that would eventually unite the entire Arab world, at least for a time.

The ancient Palestinian Jews who followed Rabbi Jesus also had real, physical enemies, people from whom they had to protect themselves, people with whom they were in daily conflict. The Roman government had taken over their land; Roman soldiers had the power to take the life of any non-Roman citizen; and some of the temple leaders even seemed to be collaborating with these foreigners, demanding more and more of the people's resources.

If we are to understand the challenging words of Jesus to love our enemies, as the people understood who first heard them, we first have to feel what it's like to have an enemy. "Enemy" is a word that we reserve today to refer to extreme cases, such as international conflicts, or to use metaphorically when speaking of people with whom we are in conflict. Some people may not feel as if they have any real enemies, even though they treat people as if they are enemies all the time.

Who are the enemies we are called to love? Are we talking about the person at home who criticizes everything we do? Are we talking about the colleague at work who fills our days with unnecessary stress and conflict? Do we turn the stranger who cuts us off in traffic into an enemy, at least for a few minutes of rage? Do unknown members of groups that do not share our beliefs or political opinions, or that seem to threaten our welfare and communities, suddenly become our enemy?

Sociologists have long contended that societies look for a shared enemy in order to empower people to rally together against a common foe. Our "enemy" is that person whom we struggle or rage against, whether it is a family member, friend, acquaintance, or stranger.

The Greek language has many words for "love" depending on the particular relationship or type of love. For instance, Greek uses the word *philos* for familial love and *eros* for physical, sensual love. In Greek, the word Rabbi Jesus uses when he says "love your enemy" is *agapate*, literally "to be loving" from the root *agape*.

---

18. Nasr, *Quran*, 158–59.

Worldly Wisdom and Foolish Grace

Agape refers to a deep, unconditional, spiritual love, or the way in which God loves—the highest form of love. *Agape* is not merely an emotion or feeling but includes the will to do what is best for the other person. *Agape* is love as an active verb, especially when the word is used in the active present tense, as it is used when Rabbi Jesus says, "Love your enemies."

It is nearly impossible to simply decide to change the way one feels, to control or change our emotions simply because we want to, but to love our enemies with *agape* love does not mean that we like them or condone their behavior, but that we *respond* to them lovingly, "as if" we feel love toward them. *Agape* love requires separating the person from their behaviors. We are called to treat our enemies "as if" they are beloved with understanding, gentleness, patience, and kindness, until our love for them becomes real.

We are not called to approve of or accept bad behavior. Scripture is clear that God hates wrong doing, injustice, and all other forms of evil and calls us to fight against such actions. Loving our enemy means that we learn to see beyond disagreements, conflicts, and even beyond injustice—ours and other's—to see human beings as created by God and to treat them as such. It is in this type of relationship that miraculous change happens.

To love someone who reacts abusively toward us is perhaps the most challenging of all the teachings of Abraham's Tent. It requires great courage, humility, and understanding. Martin Luther King, Jr. , Mahatma Gandhi, and Nelson Mandela, three of the great prophetic peacemakers of our time, found ways to love those who persecuted others. For these peacemakers, loving the enemy meant going to the enemy, sitting with them, meeting them as a fellow child of God, to begin the work of transformation and reconciliation.

We are called to trust that there is something in our enemy that God loves and therefore we can love. We learn to love our enemies in order to transform ourselves. When we are transformed, our adversaries, relationships, and communities are transformed. Love, nonviolence, humility, trust, and perseverance are the forces that have given power to struggles for peace and justice throughout human history.

Perhaps Rabbi Jesus argues in this lesson that we are to love enemies in order to *be* children of God, in order to *be* part of God's creation. We are called to love enemies in order to *be* children of the God who causes the sun to rise on the evil and on the good and who sends rain on the righteous and on the unrighteous. We are called to *be* children of the God who blesses both the righteous and the unrighteous with loving families, food to eat, security and health.

The Apostle Paul wrote to the Church in Ephesus that they were to be imitators of God and live in love as Christ loved us. (Eph 5:1) We live in love when we treat enemies with understanding and compassion, when we treat those who approach us with anger, hatred, insult, and injustice, as creations of God. Rabbi Jesus knew that we must love our enemies so that they would no longer *be* our enemies. Only a world without enemies will be the world of peace and wholeness that we are called to co-create.

9

Live Generously

One man gives generously and ends with more:
Another stints on doing the right things and incurs a loss.

Proverbs 11:24[1]

As he was setting out on a journey, a man ran up and knelt before him, and asked him, "Good Teacher, what must I do to inherit eternal life?" Jesus said to him, "Why do you call me good? No one is good but God alone. You know the commandments: You shall not murder; You shall not commit adultery; You shall not steal; You shall not bear false witness; You shall not defraud; Honor your father and mother." He said to him, "Teacher, I have kept all these since my youth." Jesus, looking at him, loved him and said, "You lack one thing; go, sell what you own, and give the money to the poor, and you will have treasure in heaven; then come, follow me." When the man heard this, he was shocked and went away grieving, for he had many possessions.

Then Jesus looked around and said to his disciples, "How hard it will be for those who have wealth to enter the kingdom of God!" And the disciples were perplexed at these words. But Jesus said to them again, "Children, how hard it is to enter the kingdom of God! It is easier for a camel to go through the eye of a needle than for someone who is rich to enter the kingdom of God." They were greatly astounded and said to one another, "Then who can be saved?" Jesus

1. Pelican, *Sacred*, 1303.

looked at them and said, "For mortals it is impossible, but not for God; for God all things are possible."

MARK 10:17–27

It is not piety to turn your faces toward the east and west. Rather, piety is he who believes in God, the Last Day, the angels, the Book, and the prophets; and who gives wealth, despite loving it, to kinsfolk, orphans, the indigent, the traveler, beggars, and for [the ransom of] slaves; and performs the prayer and gives the alms; and those who fulfill their oaths when they pledge them, and those who are patient in misfortune, hardship, and moments of peril. It is they who are the sincere, and it is they who are the reverent.

QURAN 2:117[2]

WORLDLY WISDOM—"YOU WORK HARD FOR YOUR MONEY"

Consumerism, Charity, and Tax Reform

Most people are uncomfortable when it comes to talking about money, especially *their* money. How much income we make, how much we have in the bank, how much money we spend, how we spend it, and how much money we give away are topics almost as private and potentially embarrassing as our age, weight, or sex lives.

People may feel judged by those who have more or less money than they have, or they may feel guilty themselves to have more money than some people and jealous of the people who have more than they have. We have a hard time developing a healthy relationship with money.

It doesn't help the matter that most cultures feel that money is private and no one should tell anyone else how to spend it. Worldly wisdom also encourages us at times, to think that those who are poor are lazy or simply not smart enough to make more money. Worldly wisdom will try to teach us: "Those people just need to get a job like the rest of us!"

Except for a few decades when "flower children" preached peace, love, and the ideal of communal living, our recent history has seen a slow,

---

2. Nasr, *Quran*, 76.

consistent decline in the ideal of shared resources and an increase in the ideal of capitalism and everyone's right to earn and spend as they choose.

Our ancestors who lived in small towns and villages or spread across acres of farmland knew that folks had to work together when times were hard. When a neighbor's barn burned down, everyone came from miles around for a community "barn rising," knowing that their neighbor would do the same for them. I remember when my mother would take food to families struggling with health issues, grieving the death of a loved one, or suddenly unable to work. Borrowing your neighbor's lawnmower, ladder, or "cup of sugar" was common place not so long ago, but I can't imagine asking for such a favor of my neighbors these days.

What criteria do we use when making financial decisions? If we have an expense budget, those items that provide safety, shelter, and nourishment for the household probably take precedence. On the other hand, some people don't budget at all, assuming that there will always be enough money to pay the bills or because they simply pay bills as they come and quit spending when the money runs out.

People fall prey to the temptations of spending beyond their budget. We are bombarded by commercial messages that influence us to think that the best way of expressing our love during times of celebration is by giving the biggest and most sought after gifts, regardless of how much we can realistically afford to spend. Worldly wisdom teaches us to love family and friends by giving them something special which often equates with something expensive.

The message of most consumer advertising is that if *you* want to be loved by others, you should spend your money on products that will make you more loveable, i.e., make you look younger, more beautiful, and will allow you to fit in with the other beautiful and loveable people of the world.

Consumerism also convinces us that we can overcome our worries and problems by purchasing things created to make life easier. Our neighbors seem to be happy when their kids are bouncing on the new trampoline in their backyard. Yet we hardly notice when that trampoline sits empty during wet and cold months, often covered with leaves and forgotten toys—instead of bouncing children.

The family seemed excited when they came home with a new motor boat, but now it sits parked in the driveway, as they complain about how little free time they have from work. The neighbors seem to have everything they could ever want, but are heard fighting with each other, or are seen sitting alone on the patio looking at their cellphone for hours. Garages are packed to the brim with things that people hardly ever use and boxes with "who knows what?" inside. Warehouse sized storage facilities are built for those things that people might need "someday" or cannot bear to part with, and people pay to store what they cannot fit into their living situations.

Consumerism and commercialism has left many of us with more than we need, more than we have room for, and more credit card debt than we swore we'd ever accumulate. All of this "more" is the source of stress, worry, and unhappiness which leads to more accumulating. We've created a vicious circle which causes unhappy and unhealthy lifestyles.

Money and power go hand in hand. Leaders, politicians, corporate executives, and pop stars not only make the most money but carry the most influence in our societies. Social media follows people with the most influence for those are the people we most "need" to keep track of. Our desire to keep track of them circles around giving them more influence—#bloggers #tweeting #realitytv—and therefore greater wealth and power.

Generosity has become a difficult value to cultivate with all the other financial temptations and struggles. Many feel they just don't have enough money to help others. People are told they should have "reserve funds" but feel they have no extra funds to reserve. What responsibility do people today have to help those less fortunate and what are the limits of that responsibility? How much giving seems appropriate? What is enough?

Cultivating an ethic of charitable giving is harder than it used to be. Giving should never come out of guilt, but many people still cast a judgmental or envious eye on those who are able to hob knob at a charity event with checkbook in hand. Charitable giving today is a touchy subject. Seats at fund raising dinners are often expensive even for the middle class. Many folks today can barely pay the bills when an emergency hits. It is hard for young families or couples just starting their careers to set aside savings. Young families often have the added expense of raising children or trying to balance work with personal self-care, enrichment, and relaxation. Expenses for continuing education are beyond what many can realistically afford.

Some people are truly generous, even when it is beyond their means or when it means living with less. One should never give out of guilt; giving should never go hand in hand with feeling obligated; but we understand, when there are extra incentives, how giving naturally rises:

> Research on giving in the United States has now produced definitive empirical evidence to show a decline in the participation and

amounts donated by "small" and "medium" (actually, median) donors and an increasing reliance on "large" donors. That lead sentence should make every reader stop and envision the future of philanthropy in our democracy.

... There are two seemingly unrelated trends that are both affecting the nature of how America gives. The growth in total giving and total giving by households is to be chronicled and celebrated; however, while I do not share the antipathy expressed by some toward large gifts from wealthy and high-income donors, I am concerned about the causes and the effects of the loss of gifts from lower and middle-income households. This makes our philanthropic sector less vibrant as well as less reflective of our overall society, thereby diminishing our civil discourse and civil society generally.

But there is one policy proposal that would likely attenuate the decline of the small donor: reinstate the universal charitable deduction for all households, regardless of whether or not they itemize deductions. This would provide incentives to all to give and reinforce our philanthropic values in the tax code—for one and all, regardless of income level. This measure was a part of the federal income tax code from 1982 through 1986, so it is hardly uncharted territory—and it is well past time that the sector gets firmly behind it.[3]

Universal charitable deductions are only part of our need for tax reform. The 2016 US presidential campaign promised tax reforms that would benefit those people in need. What actually changed, once the election was over, however, was not as encouraging as the promises made. The wealthiest US citizens still pay a lower percentage of their income in taxes than any other group of citizens.

FOOLISH GRACE—"LIVE GENEROUSLY"

Mark 10:17–27

As he was setting out on a journey, a man ran up and knelt before him, and asked him, "Good Teacher, what must I do to inherit eternal life?" Jesus said to him, "Why do you call me good? No one is good but God alone. You know the commandments: You shall not murder; You shall not commit adultery; You shall not steal; You shall not bear false witness; You shall not defraud; Honor your

---

3. Rooney, "The Growth," para 1.

father and mother." He said to him, "Teacher, I have kept all these since my youth." Jesus, looking at him, loved him and said, "You lack one thing; go, sell what you own, and give the money to the poor, and you will have treasure in heaven; then come, follow me."

When the man heard this, he was shocked and went away grieving, for he had many possessions. Then Jesus looked around and said to his disciples, "How hard it will be for those who have wealth to enter the kingdom of God!" And the disciples were perplexed at these words. But Jesus said to them again, "Children, how hard it is to enter the kingdom of God! It is easier for a camel to go through the eye of a needle than for someone who is rich to enter the kingdom of God." They were greatly astounded and said to one another, "Then who can be saved?" Jesus looked at them and said, "For mortals it is impossible, but not for God; for God all things are possible."

This lesson from Rabbi Jesus is set within a sequence of stories that begins with the story of the rabbi welcoming children. (See Chapter 2) The rabbi rebukes the disciples for trying to turn parents and their children away saying to them, "Do not hinder the children from coming to me" and then adds, "to such belongs the kingdom of God." (Mark 10:14) Rabbi Jesus acts as if children know all that anyone needs to know about the kingdom of God.

Immediately following the story of the children, Rabbi Jesus is approached by a man (the *opposite* of a child) with a question about Eternal Life. Jewish author Levine explains that "eternal life" is life with God, the only eternal being and, at least, in this instance this phrase should be equated with the kingdom of God.[4] Again, Rabbi Jesus is teaching his followers how to enter the kingdom of God.

This lesson is commonly called the story of The Rich, Young Ruler. Actually, only Matthew calls the man who comes to Rabbi Jesus "young" (Matt 19:20) and only Luke calls him a "ruler." (Luke 18:18) The gospel writers all agreed, however, that the man was rich.

The question that Rabbi Jesus was asked this time was one that rabbis were often asked: "Good Teacher, what must I do to have eternal life?" Notice how the verbs have changed with the adult's question? Also, though Rabbi Jesus had said that children would "enter" the kingdom, the rich man asks about *inheriting* or *having* the kingdom.

In Luke, when the question was asked by a lawyer, Rabbi Jesus responded saying, "What is written in the law? What do you find there?" The

---

4. Levine, *Misunderstood*, 81.

lawyer answered, "You shall love the LORD your God with all your heart, and with all your soul, and with all your strength, and with all your mind; and your neighbor as yourself." Rabbi Jesus said to the lawyer, "You have given the right answer; do this, and you will live." (Luke 10:25–37) The lawyer, however, decided he needed clarification about *who* qualified as his neighbor, at which point Rabbi Jesus told him a parable about a good Samaritan. (Luke 10:30–37)

Even though the rich man in this lesson claims to have followed all those commandments since he was *young*, (perhaps another subtle reminder of Jesus and the children) Rabbi Jesus tells him he is still lacking one thing. Even though he is not killing, stealing, defrauding, committing adultery or bearing false witness, even though he honors his mother and father, he is still not reaching the kingdom. Rabbi Jesus says, "You lack one thing. Go, sell all you have, and give the money to the poor and you will have treasure in heaven. Then come and follow me." (Mark 10:21)

For Rabbi Jesus to take the extreme position of teaching that everything one possessed, 100% of one's possessions, should be sold and the money given to the poor, sent the rich man looking for a second opinion. This was not exactly the answer that he had hoped for. To the lawyer in Luke, Rabbi Jesus taught the compassion of a good Samaritan but to the rich man in this lesson from Mark, Jesus said, "How hard it is for those who have wealth to enter the kingdom of God. Indeed it is easier for a camel to go through the eye of a needle." (Mark 10:24-25)

"The eye of a needle" was a common euphuism for "a very small opening." Metaphors about animals going through the "eye of a needle" were common in first century Judea. The Babylonian Talmud uses this graphic exaggeration when speaking about the rational aspect of dreams, saying, "(Dreams) do not show a man a palm tree of gold, nor an elephant going through the eye of a needle."[5]

The Jesus Seminar scholars attribute this phrase directly to Rabbi Jesus because it presents a "humorous hyperbole more likely to have come from Jesus than from a more serious–minded follower of his."[6] In true human fashion, most of the energy that biblical translators and scholars have given to this lesson over the years, has been in attempting to "soften" it.

Some console themselves with the fact that there were small gates in the wall around Jerusalem that were called an "Eye of the Needle" gate.

---

5. Epstein, "Sanhedrin," Berakoth, 55b.
6. Funk, *Five Gospels*, 92.

Live Generously

Some of these narrow gates still exist. They were created to make it difficult for people to enter the city after the main gates were closed at night. They allowed only one person to pass through at a time, not with much baggage, and were a necessary defense system against invaders. These narrow gates were easily guarded by one soldier.

Some scholars suggest that Rabbi Jesus may have been referring to an actual sewing needle and that the word Jesus used instead of "camel" could have been "ship's rope." The two words sound and look similar in Greek. They assume that the exaggeration of a rope going through the eye of a needle makes more sense than a camel trying to do that. Getting a ship's rope through the eye of a needle was a translation that didn't work for most other editors—I'd venture to guess—because it gave no "wiggle room" for the wealthy, in their interpretation of the parable.

A softening of the parable may have been added by the interpretations Mark and other gospel writers gave. All three gospels give readers some reassurance just in case getting through the eye of the needle sounds far too impossible for those with wealth. All three record that when the disciples asked Jesus, "Then who can be saved?" Rabbi Jesus said, "For mortals it's impossible, but not for God; after all, everything's possible for God."[7] (Mark 10:26-27)

Torah describes the way God's people are expected to handle their wealth and possessions. Observing Torah makes it difficult to get rich, especially if you do not have much wealth in the first place. Torah says that you cannot charge interest if you are able to loan money to someone. (Exo:22:25)

Torah also teaches that if you buy land from a desperately poor neighbor, you have to allow that person to buy that land back for the cost you paid for it instead of trying to make a profit. (Lev 25:25-28) Torah commands that you leave a portion of your field, the leftover grain from your harvest, and some of the fruit on your vines, every year, for the poor to come and take for themselves. (Lev 19:9-10) The Torah is very egalitarian when it comes to material possessions.

A dear friend, also a pastor, once tried to say something to a couple, as he was marrying them, about how they should "bake bread together" but instead got a bit tongue-tied and said they should "break the bed together." Ever since he told me that story, I have had to carefully pause during the communion liturgy to ensure that I say "break the *bread*," rather

---

7. Funk, *Five Gospels*, 92.

than "break the *bed!* Recently, the phrase "eye of the needle" was similarly altered in my brain when another friend said to me that doing something was "as hard as going through the eye of the *camel*." Now I have to be careful with that phrase also.

This lesson from Rabbi Jesus about the "eye of a needle" is another one of his most difficult teachings, such as "love your enemies" and "turn the other cheek." In fact, it may be his hardest teaching, because it "messes" with our money. Commentators or preachers who soften the blow by proposing that a very small and agile camel might actually have been able to squeeze through such a gate or by pointing out that if the camel "lightened its load," as Rabbi Jesus told the rich man to do, it would have been even easier to enter, are not doing anyone any favors.

Their interpretation just fits better with our preferred theology of God's grace. Their interpretation might be so much better that we might go right on accumulating things, trusting that there is a loophole through which we can squeeze. The common discussion around this text is: "Just how difficult do you think Rabbi Jesus said it was going to be to enter the kingdom?" We typically do not go anywhere near the actual issue of accumulating wealth or living generously.

Becoming like children seemed like a hard task—especially without any clear directions as to what that might look like. Entering the kingdom through the narrow gate seems equally inconvenient and cumbersome. The lawyer of Luke hoped that loving God and helping a few of his neighbors was enough. The rich man in Mark hoped that being a law abiding citizen would be enough to insure his eternal life.

This is where we get stuck. If we just lead a life following the basic rules of morality that everyone has agreed upon, isn't that enough? If God is truly as gracious as we believe, gracious enough to forgive all our sins, why would the kingdom of God be so difficult to enter? Why was Rabbi Jesus always taking everything to the extreme?

In the tenth century BCE, King Solomon united the kingdoms of Judah and Israel. Solomon was remembered as a wise leader whose judgements brought forth deep truths. In the book of Proverbs, which is written in the form of short oracles or allegories, Solomon is credited as saying, "One man gives generously and ends with more: Another stints on doing the right things and incurs a loss." (Prov 11:24)

Some preachers, doing their best to encourage a growth in financial giving from their parishioners for church operations, have interpreted this proverb to their congregation as meaning that if you give generously to others, more money will come back to you; in other words, the more you give, the more you will receive. It is more likely that, as an allegory, the proverb was meant to teach that those who are generous receive riches of far greater value than money, such as contentment, joy, wisdom, and less attachment to material wealth. Generosity that is unconditional, that does not expect something in return, can bring someone to change their perspectives on what has true value.

The Prophet Muhammad recited several messages from Allah regarding generosity:

> It is not piety to turn your faces toward the east and west. Rather, piety is he who believes in God, the Last Day, the angels, the Book, and the prophets; and who gives wealth, despite loving it, to kinsfolk, orphans, the indigent, the traveler, beggars, and for [the ransom of] slaves; and performs the prayer and gives the alms; and those who fulfill their oaths when they pledge them, and those who are patient in misfortune, hardship, and moments of peril. It is they who are the sincere, and it is they who are the reverent. (Quran 2:117)

After leaving Mecca to settle at Medina, those who followed Muhammad observed that Jews prayed facing to the west and Christians prayed facing eastward.[8] Having been raised by a tribe who shunned empty religious rituals and ostentation, Muhammad heard the Lord calling him to strive toward holding deeper values in the way they treated others. "Faith in God, the Last Day, the angels, the book, and the prophets" are the five principles of Islam with which the Prophet described Islam to the archangel Gabriel.[9]

In the phrase "give wealth, despite loving it," the word "despite" could be referring to the fact that they are willing to give from their wealth, despite needing the resource to escape their own poverty or for their own basic needs, despite desiring all the things that the money could buy for them, or despite not being able to live without the lifestyle their wealth provides. In other words: "Those who have so much money to spare that money has come to mean nothing to them, are not honored as greatly for they are only giving away that which has little value to them."

---

8. Nasr, *Quran*, 75.
9. Nasr, *Quran*, 75.

The list of those who are to receive our generosity includes the most vulnerable in society, the poorest of the poor, the orphans, the indigent, beggars, and slaves. There is an equalizing of wealth being called for in this message. And yet, we are also not to forget those who we might most begrudge the generosity, our own relatives, who we are most familiar with and may be quickest to judge as unworthy or undeserving.

Some people listen to Rabbi Jesus saying "sell all you have and give to the poor" with the ears of those who have more than most of the people on this planet. These people still struggle with wanting more, that "new car" or "bigger house in a nicer neighborhood," or wanting to be able to send their kids to "the most prestigious college." "Selling all you have and giving the money to the poor," sounds unreasonable even to those who have more than their share of the world's wealth.

Now listen, if you will, with the ears of one of the peasants who might have stood just behind the rich man as Rabbi Jesus spoke. "Yes, you heard him. Sell all you have, rich man!" the poor woman may have thought to herself. A poor fisherman may have thought, "You who are so rich should just try to live for a few days with as little as we have, with nothing but the shirt on your back and the fish roasting on your fire. Maybe then you would find the treasure of the kingdom everywhere you look."

"Who is a wealthy person?" asked the Jewish sages in the Mishnah, and their answer was: "One who is happy with his portion." The Mishnah, first century CE commentary on Torah, advises that if one is not happy with what they presently have, then further material possessions will not increase their level of happiness.[10]

The point is not that we just sell everything and give all our money to the poor, but that learning to live without all the luxuries that we think are so important, even if it means actually giving those things away, is the only way to be more appreciative of life's true gifts and more compassionate toward those in need. For those who have become dependent on so much material wealth, living without may be the only way to find the true treasures of life. The more we who are encumbered by "things" go without, the more we might be able to see what we still have in a new light, in the light of abundance and blessing and opportunity. Then, and only then, will we live generously toward others.

The Prophet Muhammad was quite adamant when instructing others to give generously and knew well the dangers of a wealthy life:

---

10. Chabad, "Ethics," 4:1, para 3.

Live Generously

If someone is given wealth by God but does not pay the welfare tax, his wealth will be represented to him on the Day of Resurrection as a viper encircling him, striking him with two streams of poison. It will seize him by the jaws and will say, "I am your wealth; I am your hoard."[11]

---

11. Cleary, *Wisdom*, 37.

10

Let Your Light Shine

For the commandment is a lamp,
The teaching is a light.
And the way to life is the rebuke that disciplines.

PROVERBS 6: 23[1]

He said to them, "Is a lamp brought in to be put under the bushel basket, or under the bed, and not on the lamp stand? For there is nothing hidden, except to be disclosed; nor is anything secret, except to come to light. Let anyone with ears to hear listen!"

MARK 4: 21–23

And unto God is the journey's end. Not equal are the blind and the seeing, nor the darkness and the light, not the shade and scorching heat. Not equal are the living and the dead. Truly God causes whomsoever He will to hear, but thou canst not cause those in graves to hear. Thou are naught but a warner. Truly We have sent thee with the truth as a bearer of glad tidings and as a warner. And there has been no community but that a warner has passed among them.

QURAN 35:18E–24[2]

    1. Pelikan, *Sacred*, 1294.
    2. Nasr, *Quran*, 1061.

WORLDLY WISDOM—"KEEP YOUR THOUGHTS TO YOURSELVES"

Privacy, Freedoms, and Speaking Up

With the excuse of being courteous, civil, good-mannered, and even kind and gentle, "worldly wisdom" would have us believe that we should keep our thoughts, ideas, feelings, and especially moral values to ourselves. It is "politically correct" these days to be tolerant of the thoughts and feelings of others and not to speak about controversial political issues in groups with diverse opinions, especially if the group includes your family or friends. Everyone has a right to their own opinion, society claims and laws enforce, as long as those opinions are not harming others. The only thing we do *not* feel required to tolerate these days is *intolerance*.

Everyone values their privacy and no one wants to be preached at by those who think differently than they do. The Golden Rule has been stretched to remind us to keep our thoughts to ourselves as we would like others to keep their thoughts to themselves. Religious beliefs are often the most important of all the issues people feel should remain private. The freedoms declared in the US Constitution, especially the Freedom of Religion and Freedom of Speech, are held dear by US citizens.

Some of these constitutional freedoms, however, could stand in opposition to other freedoms. Some religious beliefs expect their followers to convert others to their religion. The so called Great Commissioning (Matt 28:19) calls all followers of Rabbi Jesus to: "Go therefore and make disciples of all nations, baptizing them ... and teaching them to obey everything that I have commanded you."

Many Christians have perverted the justice and compassion of the gospel while forcing their "one, true" religion on others. The Crusaders used lethal force in trying to convert non-believers who held land of which they wished to take possession. In the Doctrine of Discovery, the Church gave Christian explorers the right to convert or take the lands of non-Christians even if it meant using lethal force.

Most Christians today, embarrassed and dismayed by hostile and hateful evangelism, have decided that they should keep their religious beliefs to themselves. It is as if they have hidden their religious and moral values in a closet or under the bed along with the power of their faith, so as not to offend others.

"Worldly wisdom" claims that it can be prideful, self-centered, and sometimes dangerous to call attention to ourselves. Many people are convinced that there are people waiting "out there" to take advantage of them and, therefore, that they should keep their thoughts to themselves.

Many churches follow this "worldly wisdom" by steering clear of certain subject matters that are considered "political" during sermons or classes or anything sponsored by the church. "Politics doesn't belong in church," minsters are told when they speak about an issue of injustice, as if those topics are "off-limits" when it comes to matters of faith, as if those are political rather than moral issues. Much of the moral outrage that people of faith speak against with compassion for the oppressed gets ignored by the news until a church speaks out against such compassion.

Religious groups around the world are losing followers. Advances in science and technology are over-shadowing the ancient wisdom of faith communities. The wisdom of faith must not remain hidden behind locked church doors for fear of intruders. The wisdom of faith must not be clutched tightly away from diverse, interfaith voices for fear of contamination by new and challenging words, images, and understandings.

Shining from most of our hilltops today are the devouring fires of greed and fear instead of the lights of compassion and equality. The sparkle of wealth, consumerism, and personal pleasure blinds us from the brilliance of the stardust that shines within all creation.

FOOLISH GRACE—"LET YOUR LIGHT SHINE"

Mark 4:21–23

> He said to them, "Is a lamp brought in to be put under the bushel basket or under the bed, and not on the lamp stand? For there is nothing hidden, except to be disclosed; nor is anything secret, except to come to light. Let anyone with ears to hear listen!"

The rhetorical question, "Is a lamp brought in to be put under the bushel basket?" was a common aphorism in Rabbi Jesus' day. Used often enough, these common sayings became what the people most often remembered from their teachers.

"Hiding light" is an oxymoron. Light is useless when it is hidden, it might as well be darkness. The very nature of light, what light *is*, the character of light, disappears if it is covered up. Why bother lighting a lamp if you're going to cover it with a basket or put it under the bed? You might as well blow out the lamp.

Some version of this saying about not covering the light is found in each of the synoptic gospels where it is taught by Rabbi Jesus in different contexts. In each case, however, the basic lesson remains the same, "Do not hide your light!"

As children, some of us learned to sing, "This little light of mine, I'm gonna let it shine." No one ever explained to me what the light was, so I assumed that it was *my* light, *my* personality, *my* goodness. I was supposed to let *my* light shine so that others could see how great *I* was. The gospel writers used this saying to speak of the light of God that fills each of us. The light of God is the light with which we view the world and discern good from evil.

Matthew uses the "light under a bushel" lesson following Rabbi Jesus' teaching on "The Beatitudes," (Matt 5:3–12) and combines it with a paraphrase of the lesson from Rabbi Jesus about seasoning every sacrifice with salt. (Matt 5:13) Rabbi Jesus taught that those who were "blessed" in God's new community were those who were poor in spirit, those who mourned, those who were meek, those who hungered and thirsted for righteousness, those who were merciful, those who were pure in heart, and those who were peacemakers. Jesus spoke directly to the crowd when he ended by saying, "And blessed are *you* when people hate and persecute you because of me." Matthew follows these words of blessing from Rabbi Jesus with the rabbi's words about light:

> You are the light of the world. A city built on a hill cannot be hid. No one after lighting a lamp puts it under the bushel basket, but on the lampstand, and it gives light to all in the house. In the same way, let your light shine before others, so that they may see your good works and give glory to your Father in heaven.(Matt 5:14–16)

In Matthew, light represents the wisdom and compassion of God that is evident in the "good works" of those whom Rabbi Jesus calls "blessed." The image of a light "on a hill" was aimed at the disciples as a community, rather than as individuals, and used by Matthew to speak directly to the early Christian church as it developed.

Matthew's gospel was written after the fall of Jerusalem and destruction of the Temple in 70 CE. Matthew was written to a minority within the Jewish community who may have worried that they could not hold on to their experience of Rabbi Jesus in the midst of a fledgling reformation

Worldly Wisdom and Foolish Grace

toward rabbinic Judaism. Matthew's use of the light metaphor reminded this small band of followers that Rabbi Jesus called his disciples "light for the world, like a city built on a hill."

In Luke, this light fills the body when the "eye," the "lamp of the body," is healthy. When the eye is not healthy, the body is full of darkness. (Luke 11:34)

Luke uses the phrase "light under a bushel" twice. The saying is used, first of all, in the same context that Mark uses it, as part of an explanation of the purpose of parables. (Luke 8:16–17) Then, a few chapters later, (Luke 11:33–36) this saying is used again after Rabbi Jesus teaches that "those who are blessed are those who hear the word of God and obey it." (Luke 11:28)

Rabbi Jesus calls the present generation "evil" for wanting yet another sign, saying that the Sign of Jonah was the only sign they would be given. We can only imagine how tired Rabbi Jesus must have been of his followers asking again and again for some kind of magic sign from God. "At the final judgement," Jesus reminds them, "the people of Nineveh would be allowed to stand up and condemn the people because Nineveh repented when Jonah came to warn them, while the present generation waited until the final judgement for another sign from God. (Luke 11:29–32)

Then Jesus declares,

> No one after lighting a lamp puts it in the cellar, but on the lampstand so that those who enter may see the light. Your eye is the lamp of your body. If your eye is healthy, your whole body is full of light; but if it is not healthy, your body is full of darkness. If then your whole body is full of light, with no part of it in darkness, it will be as full of light as when a lamp gives you light with its rays. (Luke11:33–36)

In Greek, the word translated as "healthy" means literally "non-compound," in other words, "single, simple, sincere, clear, or sound." The King James Bible chose to use the word "single." Hal Taussig's "A New New Testament" translates the word as "unclouded."[3]

The Peshita translation from Aramaic gives further *illumination* of the Luke 11:34–36 text, translating it as,

> The lamp of your body is your eye. Therefore when your eye is true all your body will also be bright. But if it should be evil, your body will also be dark. Take heed therefore lest the light that is in

---

3. Taussig, *A New*, 107.

you is darkness. And if all your body is light and does not have any portion of darkness in it, all of it will be enlightened as a lamp, by its flame, enlightens you.[4]

The Peshita translation says that when the "eye" is true the whole body will be *bright* (i.e., filled with light) and that if the eye is evil the whole body will be *dark*. Perhaps our eye becomes *clouded* when our perception is distorted by cultural misunderstandings, prejudices, or fears. A flashlight that does *not* have a cloudy lens illumines more clearly than one *with* a cloudy lens. We know that some people seem to "see" the light of God and yet, because of their cloudy or confused perception or intentions, the light becomes darkened.

In Mark, the light of God is equated with understanding. Mark inserts this saying directly after his interpretation of the Parable of the Sower. Mark believes that the Parable of the Sower is about how people understand God's will and way differently. Mark writes that, hearing the parables of Rabbi Jesus, some will look and not see, some will listen and not hear, and some may even not understand at first but turn around and come back later when they've figured it out. (Mark 4:10–12)

Mark believes that the Parable of the Sower teaches that sometimes our understanding of God disappears; sometimes our wisdom withers when troubles arise; and sometimes our worldly cares and temptations choke our ability to see truth. Even so, Rabbi Jesus insists that some understanding of God's kingdom will eventually grow as long as we keep sowing seeds. (Mark 4:13–20)

As Mark reflected on the Parable of the Sower he also remembered that Jesus had said:

> Is a lamp brought in to be put under the bushel basket, or under the bed, and not on the lampstand? For there is nothing hidden except to be disclosed; nor is anything secret, except to come to light. Let anyone with ears to hear listen! (Mark 4:21–23)

Rabbi Jesus knew that it didn't make any more sense to hide the love and grace of God than it makes to cover light with a basket. Just as light is necessary to illumine a room, the love of God is needed to reveal the will of God toward justice and compassion.

Mark expands the light metaphor by assuring us that, "there is nothing hidden, except to be disclosed; nor is anything secret, except to come to

---

4 Younan, "Peshitta."

light." The Jesus Seminar scholars claim that this additional verse 24 seems "garbled" because "people do not generally hide things in order to make them known."[5] Yet it could be that Mark meant that such wisdom would not and could not be hidden for long and that, ultimately, in the fullness of time, everything that is a mystery to us now will be revealed.

In the second story of creation in Genesis, Adam and Eve "see" God telling them not to eat of the "Tree of the Knowledge of Good and Evil." Because their understanding is clouded, Adam and Eve "see" a wise serpent who is deceiving them, telling them that God has told them not to eat of that tree so that they will not become as powerful as God. In their confusion, they are filled with darkness and choose poorly. (Gen 2:15–25)

There are those who speak eloquent words of faith, seeming to be part of God's light, claiming to live their lives in obedience to God, yet whose lives may eventually reveal evidence of dark intentions, self-centeredness, and greed. The light of God, which seemed to fill them at times, may eventually be seen as the darkness of greed and apathy.

Rabbi Jesus teaches, "Take heed, lest the light that is in you is darkness," teaching that self-examination, honesty and humility will lead to examining our motives more carefully. Our whole body (i.e., soul or life) will be filled with the light of God when our perception is not clouded. When the eye is seeing truly, and God's wisdom is evident, when the right way of living in relationship with God and others is clear to us, we will be filled with God's light.

Rabbi Jesus remembered the Prophet Isaiah's words from Torah, "Your light has come and the glory of the LORD has risen upon you. Nations shall come to your light and kings to the brightness of your dawn." (Isaiah 60:1–3) The light that had come was God's love and compassion.

It is hard for us to imagine why Rabbi Jesus would have used such high praise for the crowds that followed him. Light for the World? Hardly! They were mostly peasant farmers, fishermen, craftsmen, women and children. These were powerless people that Rabbi Jesus himself described as poor in spirit, mournful, and meek. They were not exactly what most people would describe as "a city built on a hill."

Why, in God's name, would Rabbi Jesus consider them "blessed," "salt of the earth," and "the light of the world?" I expect they didn't feel very "blessed," a word which translates better as "fortunate," in this case. Perhaps

---

5. Funk, *Five Gospels*, 57.

Let Your Light Shine

Rabbi Jesus considered them fortunate because they were *already* living as part of God's beloved community.

Would these people have considered themselves "salt of the earth?" Salt, after all, was considered a very valuable and essential commodity in their day and culture. Surely they did not feel very valuable or essential, but Rabbi Jesus called them "salt," none-the-less, perhaps because they were learning to temper the flames of their passion with compassion. (See Chapter 5)

What had the crowd around Jesus done to increase their community's understanding, to enlighten or educate others? Perhaps Rabbi Jesus saw that they were a "light on a hill" because they were filled with God's wisdom and grace as they worked together, helped each other, had compassion for one another and those in need.

Rabbi Jesus, like other Jewish mystics, taught that we were not to hide the light of God when it shines from within us. If faith is a private matter, if how faith affects our life is our business and nobody else's, we may be tempted to think that the moral values of our faith should be kept to ourselves rather than displayed through our work for justice.

We are encouraged to think that it is not appropriate to set our light, our understanding of God's will, our values and moral wisdom, upon a hill for all to see. Setting our light on a hill, taking our light out from under the bed, seems too much like evangelism and some evangelism, for good reasons, can be dangerous business.

So why did the gospel writers and Rabbi Jesus use this saying so often? "Light is not meant to be hidden under a bushel," may have been used by the early Christians to promote evangelism, to encourage sharing the good news of God's love, and to invite others to follow Christ, but it is highly unlikely that Rabbi Jesus called people to a new religion rather than to the true way of God that he sought to reveal and live. For Rabbi Jesus, discerning through the eyes of compassion was not a new religion and, for that matter, was not specific to one faith tradition.

The book of Proverbs was written to share the light of God:

> . . . written to give 'shrewdness to the simple, knowledge and prudence to the young' (1.4), and 'to make wise men wiser' (1.5). Acquiring wisdom and knowing how to avoid the pitfalls of folly lead to health and success. Although Proverbs is a practical book dealing with the art of living, it bases wisdom solidly on the fear of the LORD.

Worldly Wisdom and Foolish Grace

Chapter 6 of Proverbs is included in the section of Proverbs that speaks specifically of the "Superiority of the Way of Wisdom" (Prov 1:8—9:18)

> For the commandment is a lamp,
> The teaching is a light.
> And the way to life is the rebuke that disciplines.
> Proverbs 6: 23[6]

This proverb is not listed specifically as a saying of the wise King Solomon, to which most of the proverbs are ascribed, but could have been the saying of another teacher, who wrote in the same style as Solomon. These writings from the tenth century BCE come from the period when the kingdoms of Israel and Judah had been reunited into one kingdom.

Even a thousand years before Rabbi Jesus, there was a common wisdom saying that referred to knowledge and teachings as "a light" and "a lamp" that illumines the way to life and corrects the way one is living. Referring to the light of wisdom as something that should not be hidden under a bushel, but set on a hill or lampstand, would have seemed perfectly logical to Rabbi Jesus, who knew these wisdom sayings.

Centuries later, the Prophet Mohammad heard Allah's angel messenger telling him that he was "naught but a warner." The term "warner" is not often used as a noun, but is an appropriate word here, for it further elaborates on this lesson about letting light shine. The Quran includes a revelation in which the angel Gabriel speaks of Mohammad and others as being "warners":

> And unto God is the journey's end. Not equal are the blind and the seeing, nor the darkness and the light, nor the shade and scorching heat. Not equal are the living and the dead. Truly God causes whomsoever He will to hear, but thou canst not cause those in graves to hear. Thou are naught but a warner. Truly We have sent thee with the truth as a bearer of glad tidings and as a warner. And there has been no community but that a warner has passed among them.
> Quran 35:18e-24[7]

When the people of God are called to be "a light to the nations, "a city set upon a hill," we are being called to be "warners." Allah's angel revealed to the Prophet Mohammad that he was "naught but a warner." This is a very

---

6. Pelican, *Sacred*, 1294.
7. Nasr, *Quran*, 1061.

specific, personal call to Mohammad, but the text also teaches that *every* community has warners that "pass among them."

The messenger of Allah was not just talking about Muslim communities, but about all communities. "Warners" speak within every faith tradition (even from those with no particular faith tradition) through those with a spirit of compassion and justice.

If everyone decided that it was best to hide their light, to keep private all their understanding of how we are called to live together, where would the *warners* be? There will be false prophets, as our holy texts also warn, and it will always be up to us to choose between warners that speak truth and false warners, (conspiracy theorists come to mind, perhaps.)

In Matthew 7:15–20 Rabbi Jesus warns of ". . . false prophets who come to you in sheep's clothing but inwardly are ravenous wolves." Rabbi Jesus says that false prophets will be known "by their fruits." In Deuteronomy 18:22, Moses warns that "if a prophet speaks in the name of the LORD but the thing does not take place or prove true, it is a word that the LORD has not spoken."

Perhaps the specific religious system that an individual chooses should be a private matter, but the light of compassion and justice is not meant to be kept hidden simply because it comes from a faith tradition. If we hide what the Spirit has led us to understand, if we keep that light hidden away at home in our private closets, how will our wisdom help build a world of peace and justice?

Researchers tell us that if the world were flat, the light of one candle could be seen by the human eye at a distance of thirty miles. A light on a lamp stand or the many lights of a city on a hilltop can shine even farther, even as far as outer space. A light in a closet will not shine beyond the inside of the closet door.

What do we do to let the light of love shine? The light of love shines when we support legislative work that builds God's beloved community, when we volunteer our time and energy to take meals to the home-bound or homeless shelters, or when we visit and care for the elderly at Senior Centers. That light shines when we put our love and compassion into action.

How we let our light shine is as important as *what* we do to let light shine. The words that are spoken as we serve others, the smiles we share, and the stories we take time to listen to, have a tremendous effect on those we serve. When we understand that all people are loved by God and are equally worthy of our love, then we teach that wisdom through our actions and through our compassion.

Speaking up is a difficult thing to do. Many in our circles of family and friends do *not* want to hear that all people are equally worthy and deserving, that personal worth is *not* based on following rules or conforming. Such talk can bring conflicting perceptions and discouraging prejudices.

Self-consciousness, timidity, and other fears will tempt us to hide our light under a bushel. As Rabbi Jesus calls us to be salt of the earth, calls us to temper passion with compassion as we sacrifice ourselves for the sake of others, Rabbi Jesus also calls us to be light for the world, to let the light of understanding, the light of love, shine out and over and upon a world in desperate need of healing and understanding. The light of the world is the *foolish grace* of a compassionate Creator that is capable of standing and speaking up against the so-called *wisdom* of human understanding. Our human world is created, not perfect, but with the ability to learn and grow from our imperfections.

The light of stars that reach us from the furthest corners of the galaxies is still not as powerful as the light of love that outshines everything. Love changes everything. Love is the starlight that illuminates the darkness of worldly wisdom, wisdom which relies, more and more, on the pixels of our own devices. Remember, there is literally within every living thing a bit of stardust.

Addendum

ON JULY 17, 2020, Former US Representative John Lewis joined the exclusive heavenly fellowship of nonviolent, compassionate, "good trouble," saints and angels. With Abraham, Jesus, Mohammad, and prophets from ages past to recent days such as Mahatma Gandhi, Sojourner Truth, Martin Luther King, Jr., and Nelson Mandela, John Lewis knew that the *only* way to create the beloved community of peace and justice on earth was through a nonviolent movement of protest, such as the movement he fought for with all of his soul, mind, and body.

The Elder and Younger Testament of scripture call each of us to "love the Lord, our God, with all your heart, with all your mind, and with all your strength." This is the greatest commandment, Jews and Christians are told. The revelation of Allah's will and way to Mohammad demands the same obedience. Why? Because that is the *only* way to the peace that will redeem our lives and our world to what it was created to be and can yet, still become.

We here in Portland, Oregon have witnessed, first hand, how some people have been taught and come to believe that the violence of systems and authorities can only be overcome with violence. We have witnessed how such a return of violence only fans the flames of fear, hatred, power-over, and militaristic mindsets. We have witnessed how the message of a nonviolent protest against racism and militarism is so easily drowned out by fire crackers, throwing objects at authorities, canisters of tear gas, guns firing rubber bullets, crowds shouting and fighting back angrily against armored and armed police and federal agents and reporters who feel it is their job to report only the most sensational events.

John Lewis was honored today for having stood amongst the nonviolent freedom fighters proclaiming still that we must stand against violence and hatred even from those who claim to stand *with* ideals.

Worldly Wisdom and Foolish Grace

Sometimes, it's not enough "to agree to disagree." Sometimes, the stakes are too high. Still those under Abraham's Tent and other spiritual "tents" agree; meeting violence with more violence never achieves a lasting peace and increased understanding. War after war has been fought and won, but we still live in a world divided by fear and prejudice; worldly wisdom still tells us that the only way to insure that your side "wins" is to beat the other side down, crack their skulls, until they, hopefully, lose their voices and all hope.

The image of peaceful protesters marching two by two, hand in hand, across the, soon to be called, "John Lewis Bridge," must become our image of the righteous marching toward the beloved community. It must become the image that gives us the power to keep moving forward until the scourge, the pandemic, of racism is put behind us and all human beings are living in justice and freedom.

Bibliography

Armstrong, Karen, *Muhammad: A Prophet For Our Time*. New York: HarperCollins, 2006.
BBC Science News, *The Human Genome: Poems on the Book of Life: A poetic exploration of the mapping of the human genetic code*. https://www.thehumangenome.co.uk/THE_HUMAN_GENOME/Comparative_Genomics.html.
Borum, Randy, "Psychology of Terrorism." University of South Florida, 2004. https://www.academia.edu/177091/Psychology_of_Terrorism.
Byasee, Jason, and Greg Carey. "Seventh Sunday After the Epiphany." in *Preaching the Revised Common Lectionary: Feasting on the Word*. Year A, Vol 1, edited by Bartlett, David L. and Barbara Brown Taylor, 380–384. Louisville: Westminster John Knox, 2009.
Chabad.org. "Ethics of the Fathers: Chapter 4" para 3. www.Chabad.org/library_cdo/aid/2032/jewish/Chapter-Four.htm.
Cleary, Thomas, trans. *The Wisdom of the Prophet: Sayings of Muhammad, Selections from the Hadith*. Boston: Shambhala, 2001.
Constitutional Rights Foundation. "A History of the Death Penalty in America." https://www.crf-usa.org/images/pdf/HistoryoftheDeathPenaltyinAmerica.
Creevey, Rev. Dr. William, *We Stand By Holy Places*, used with permission.
Crossan, John Dominic. *In Parables: The Challenge of the Historical Jesus*. New York: Harper & Row, 1973.
Darley, John M. and C. Daniel Batson, of Princeton University, "From Jerusalem to Jericho: A study of Situational and Dispositional Variables in Helping Behavior." Journal of Personality and Social Psychology 1973, Vol. 27, No. J, 100–108. http://web.missouri.edu/~segerti/1000/DarleyBateson.pdf
Death Penalty Information Center, "Innocence." https://deathpenaltyinfo.org/policy-issues/innocence.
Encyclopedia Britannica. "Biblical Criticism." Britannica.com/topic/biblical-criticism.
Epstein, I. ed., "Sanhedrin" from Babylonian Talmud, Translated by Jacob Shachter and H. Freedman. www.come-and-hear.com/Sanhedrin_38.html.
———. "Sanhedrin" from Babylonian Talmud, Translated by Maurice Simon. http://www.come-and-hear.com/berakoth/berakoth_55.html#PARTb, verse 39.
Fables of Aesop, "The Three Tradesmen." https://fablesofaesop.com/the-three-tradesmen.html.
Funk, Robert W., Roy W. Hoover, and The Jesus Seminar. *The Five Gospels: What Did Jesus Really Say?* San Francisco: Harper, 1997.

Bibliography

Gilder Lehrman Institute of American History, AP US History Study Guide, "The Doctrine of Discovery.1493." https://ap.gilderlehrman.org/resource/doctrine-discovery-1493.

Grant, Elihu. "The People of Palestine: The Peasantry, life, manners, and customs of the village." Philadelphia and London: J.B Lippincot, 1921. http://archive.org/details/peoplepalestine01grangoog/page/n180/mode/2up.

Griffith, Jeremy. *The Book of Real Answers to Everything!*, 2011. Published by WTM Publishing and Communications. Available online at World Transformation Movement, https://www.humancondition.com/human-nature/.

Hertz, Dr. J. H. C. H. *The Pentateuch and Haftorahs.* London: Socino, 1960.

Holmes, Bob and Kate Douglas. "Human Nature: Six Things We All Do." New Scientist. April 18, 2012. https://www.newscientist.com/article/mg21428610-800-human-nature-being-gossipy/.

Holy Bible: New Revised Standard Version. Nashville: Thomas Nelson, 1989.

Jinkins, Michael. "With All Due Respect." in Insights: The Faculty Journal of Austin Seminary. Spring 2018. austinseminarydigital.org/collections/show/64.

Jung, Carl, "Aion" in "The Collected Works of C.G. Jung," Vol.9/2. https://archive.org/details/collectedworksof92cgju/page/10/mode/2up.

Kennard, J. Spencer. *Render to God.* New York: Oxford University Press, 1950.

Kent, Corita and Jan Stewart. *Learning By Heart: Teachings to Free the Creative Spirit.* 2nd Edition, New York: Allworth, 2008.

Levine, Amy-Jill and Marc Zvi Brettler, Eds. *The Jewish Annotated New Testament.* (NRSV) New York: Oxford University Press, 2011.

Levine, Amy-Jill. *The Misunderstood Jew.* San Francisco, HarperCollins, 2006.

Merriam-Webster, *Webster's Ninth New Collegiate Dictionary.* Springfield: Merriam-Webster, 1989.

Meyer, Marvin W. *The Secret Sayings of Jesus.* New York: Random House, 1984.

Miller, Jerry. "Child Maltreatment 2018." https://www.acf.hhs.gov/sites/default/files/cb/cm2018.pdf.

Nasr, Seyyed Hossein, Editor-in-Chief. *The Study Quran: A New Translation and Commentary.* New York: HarperCollins, 2015.

Our Children's Trust. "Frank Ackerman." July 26, 2019. https://www.ourchildrenstrust.org/frank-ackerman. Para 7–8.

Oxford, "Learner's Dictionaries," https://www.oxfordlearnersdictionaries.com/us/definition/english/zealot?q=Zealot

Oxford, "Lexico," https://www.lexico.com/en/definition/zealot.

Ozick, Cynthia. *Ruth.* In "Congregation: Contemporary Writers Read the Jewish Bible." David Rosenberg, Ed. San Diego: Harcourt Brace Jovanovich, 1987.

Pelican, Jaroslav, ed. *Judaism: The Tanakh.* Sacred Writings, Vol 1. New York: Quality Paperback Book Club, 1992.

Perkins, Pheme. *New Testament Articles, Matthew, and Mark.* The New Interpreter's Bible Commentary. Vol.VII. Nashville: Abington, 1995.

Rooney, Patrick M., "The Growth in Total Household Giving Is Camouflaging a Decline in Giving by Small and Medium Donors: What Can We Do about It?" August 27, 2019, Non Profit Quarterly, https://nonprofitquarterly.org/2018/11/21/total-household-growth-decline-small-medium-donors/.

Sacks, Jonathan. "Socialism and Fallen Donkeys." https://www.chabad.org/parshah/article_cdo/aid/4108944/jewish/Social-Capital-and-Fallen-Donkeys.htm. line 28.

Bibliography

Sagan, Carl. "Preserving & Cherishing the Earth: An Appeal for Joint Commitment in Science & Religion." Earthrenewal.org/open_letter_to_the_religious_.htm.
Scripture4All, "Greek Interliner Bible NT." https://www.scripture4all.org/OnlineInterlinear/Greek_Index.htm.
Sleeth, Matthew. *The Gospel According to the Earth*. New York: HarperCollins, 2010.
Stauffer, Ethelbert. *Christ and the Caesars*. Philadelphia: Westminster, 1955.
Talbert, Charles H. *Reading Luke: A Literary and Theological Commentary on the Third Gospel*. Macon: Smyth & Helwys, 2002.
Taussig, Hal. *A New New Testament*. Boston: Houghton Mifflin Harcourt, 2013.
Tickle, Phyllis, *Emergence Christianity: What It Is, Where It Is Going, and Why It Matters*. Grand Rapids: Baker Books, 2012.
Vermes, G. trans., "The Rules of the Community." 1QS, Col X, #18. http://ccat.sas.upenn.edu/gopher/other/courses/rels/225/Texts/1QS.
Wesley, John, Charles Bonnet, and Louis Dutens. *A Survey of the Wisdom of God in the Creation*. 3rd ed. New York: Bangs and Mason, 1823.
Wink, Walter. *The Powers that Be: Theology for a New Millennium*. New York: Doubleday, 1998.
Woodruff, Judy. "Behind the Record Number of children detained at the Mexico-US border this year." PBS News Hour, Oct. 30, 2019, https://www.pbs.org/newshour/show/behind-the-record-number-of-children-detained-at-the-u-s-mexico-border-this-year.
Wroe, Ann. *Pontius Pilate*. New York: Random House, 1999.
Younan, Paul D. "Peshita Aramaic/English Interlinear New Testament." http://www.peshita.org. 06/01/2000.
Zaslow, David. *Jesus: First Century Rabbi*. Brewster: Paraclete, 2014.
———. *Roots and Branches*. Ashland: The Wisdom Exchange, 2011.

www.ingramcontent.com/pod-product-compliance
Lightning Source LLC
Chambersburg PA
CBHW072134160426
43197CB00012B/2101